'I don't suppose you've got any of his old suits you want to get rid of...'

Published by Oldie Publications Ltd,
65 Newman Street, London W1T 3EG
Produced by James Pembroke Publishing,
90 Walcot Street, Bath BA1 5BG

© 2007 The Oldie

ISBN: 978-0-9548176-2-6

Printed by MKT Print

Acknowledgements
The Oldie would like to thank: All the writers, illustrators and cartoonists whose work is reproduced
in these pages; Alice Pitman, for her assistance in selecting the pieces for inclusion;
Diana Smith and everyone at JPP for producing such a handsome volume.

The Oldie

ANNUAL 2008

'If you're happy and you know it, clap your hands'

Terry Wogan at
the Oldie Of The
Year Awards

FOREWORD

The Oldie is that *rara avis* – a publication that 'doesn't
give a damn', possibly due to the Editor's delusion
that he bears a passing resemblance to Clark Gable.
The Oldie genuflects to nobody, nor any passing fad
– political correctness, global warming, critical paths,
compliance, diversity, get short shrift. There is no 'spin'
here, nor pomposity or self-regard. It is true to its name
– celebrating the immaturity of the mature. A magazine
that, looking back, points the way forward.

Terry Wogan

The Old Un's diary

All the news that matters. And some that doesn't

Get in touch: diary@theoldie.co.uk

Seeing orange

The recent death of Marmaduke Hussey reminded one former BBC employee of this anecdote about the great man.

Soon after 'Duke' Hussey was appointed BBC Chairman, he went to Bush House, headquarters of the BBC World Service, to meet the staff.

A timid looking member of the Thai Section waited patiently through all the heavyweight stuff to ask his question. He kept putting his

...the Directorate and others couldn't possibly think what he might have to contribute to the discussion

hand up only to be beaten by mind-numbing questions such as 'What do you see as the future direction of the BBC?' and 'Is Bush House safe in your hands because we know Mrs Thatcher appointed you?' etc.

Finally, the great man singled out the solitary Thai gentleman and, ignoring the clamouring ladder-climbers, said: 'Yes sir, you there, what is your question?'

The Thai gentleman stood

up and glanced nervously at the Directorate and others, who couldn't possibly think what he might have to contribute to the discussion.

'Why, sir... Why... [long pause] are you called Marmaduke?'

A GUIDE to state benefits available for oldies issued by Scarborough council has been flying off the shelves recently. Perhaps this was to do with its title – *Are You Getting It?*

Fearful that it may have been giving potential readers the wrong idea, its title has now sadly been changed to *Extra Money*.

Meeting Mrs T

A recent conversation with our New York correspondent revealed that in the weeks following the 11th September attacks on the World Trade Center, she and her husband had travelled to London on business. Somewhat nervous of being abroad at that time, she was relieved when the

Athenaeum Hotel where they were staying reassured her that security at the hotel was tight – as Lady Thatcher was in residence while her house was being refurbished.

An avid Anglophile, our correspondent's husband was keen to meet the Iron Lady. Very soon the couple found themselves alone in the dining room with Maggie, Denis and a couple of bodyguards. Presently, Denis left the dining room, and Maggie soon followed, saying 'Now you'll have the place all to yourselves.'

Our correspondent's husband shot out of his seat and shook Maggie by the hand: 'Lady Thatcher, we, as Americans, are proud to be allied with you, especially at this most crucial time.' He then asked, 'How do you feel about our two countries and the state of this crazy world?'

Maggie replied: 'When I was growing up – my father was a green grocer,

At night I feel so alone

In the morning I'm so glad I am

GED

Stuff and nonsense...

Not so fast, mister

'A dangerous driving charge against an armless man caught speeding while steering with his feet has been dropped by New Zealand police. But he was fined for speeding and told to get a licence. Police say that Colin Raymond Smith, 31, who was born without arms, was caught travelling at 121 km/h near Papamoa in March.'
Australian Courier Mail, 3 Sept 06.

Canine collision

In other motoring news: in Beijing, a woman's vehicle crashed into another car while she was teaching her dog to drive. Mrs Li, from Hohhot, Inner Mongolia, said that her dog 'was fond of crouching on the steering wheel and often watched her drive.'

Daily Mail good for you

'Well-off children more at risk of cancer,' screamed the front-page headline of the *Daily Mail* recently. 'Youngsters in affluent areas are more likely to develop leukaemia and other childhood cancers,' they said.

Bad news then for rich kids and maybe a small crumb of comfort for the poor for a change? But wait, what's this on page six of the self-same edition? 'Low social status can take years off your life.' Scientists have apparently discovered that being poor shortens your life significantly. So perhaps it's best to be neither rich nor poor but middle class – just like the typical *Daily Mail* reader. Phew!

Less is more

Gwen Dorling got a surprise recently when a male stripper turned up at her birthday party. 'He was a bit of all right. I enjoyed it,' remarked Gwen. She was celebrating her 102nd birthday.

'I've changed my mind, I DO want to be a burden, son'

you know – people didn't live on credit. They took responsibility for their bills.' When our American friends tried to turn the talk back to the recent terror attacks and how to cope with them, Maggie turned to the subject of real estate. The costs of renting and buying places to live have gone over the top, was what she inferred. 'The young people today are over-extending themselves without enough of an idea about the repercussions,' she said.

Was Maggie a bit dotty, going off at a tangent like that? Or was she actually perfectly sharp, avoiding at all costs a patriotic discussion with some over-enthusiastic Americans? Our correspondent wasn't sure, but suggested that perhaps they had taken up enough of her time and shouldn't impose on her any further. Maggie

fixed her with a withering look, making it clear that the Lady wasn't yet for finishing, and continued with her non-sequiturs.

AGEISM of the Month Award goes to Gavin Martin, writing in the *Independent*. Talking of Bob Dylan's guitarist, Bruce Lang-horne, he says: 'Although he turned 66 last May, he still possesses intelligence, humour, poise and playfulness.' Really? At 66? Some kind of miracle, surely.

Fowl language

From now on, visitors to the Warwickshire Animal Sanctuary in Nuneaton will have to ask staff if they wish to see, let alone hear, Barney, their resident five-year-old Macaw.

Barney's problem is that he doesn't have any respect for authority, so when dignitaries visit the sanctuary, rather than saying, 'Who's a clever

boy?', Barney's usual refrain is: 'F**k off'.

Previously owned by a long-distance lorry driver, Barney ended up at the animal sanctuary after his owner decanted to Spain.

At a recent civic bash held there, Barney told the mayor to 'f**k off', before turning to the local vicar and telling him, 'You can f**k off too'. Not to be outdone, two policemen who were attending the bash also received some verbal abuse from Barney, who called them 'wankers', before letting it be known that as far as he was concerned they could also 'f**k off'.

The good news is that all is not lost, as Barney is now undergoing a course of intensive re-education – which includes forcing him to listen to Radio 4. Let's hope he doesn't pick up any aggressive verbal habits from John Humphrys...

THIS MONTH'S Rage Against the Dying of the Light award goes to Woody Allen, who said about being 70: 'I haven't mellowed. I haven't gained any wisdom. You don't wanna get older. There's nothing going for it. You think that because your work may be seen or read after your death, that it's compensation. But it's not. Not kids, or art, or anything. There's nothing compensating about your own death.'

Voice from the Grave

14th March, 1920 (Baghdad)
'For the most part they [Shiah mujahedin] are very hostile to us, a feeling we can't alter because it's so difficult to get at them. I'm speaking of the extremists among them; there are a few with whom we are on cordial relations. Until quite recently I've been wholly cut off from them because their tenets forbid them to look upon an unveiled woman and my tenets don't permit me to veil. I think I am right there, for it would be a tacit admission of inferiority which would put our intercourse from the first out of focus. Nor is it any good trying to make friends through the women... If the women were allowed to see me they would veil before me as if I were a man.
So you see I appear to be too female for one sex and too male for the other.'
The Letters of Gertrude Bell (Vol. 2), 1927

Spotted by Rose Foot

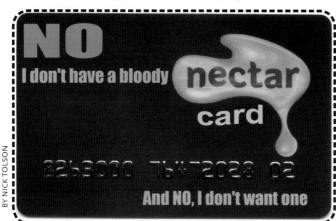

Cut out and keep for presentation to shop assistants

BY NICK TOLSON

Seeing is believing

Spotted in Virginia, USA. Submitted by R K Dillon of New York.

Miles Kington

I have a dream! About Beryl Cook's secret plot...

Along with all the other scrappy and meaningless dreams I wake up from in the morning, or at least which seem meaningless as soon as I wake up, I do sometimes have sheer action drama dreams. Really exciting James Bond-type dreams, which I have enjoyed so much up to that point that I try to get to sleep again to see what happens next – whether I shall catch up with that burglar, or escape the enemy, or get across the canyon which is between me and freedom.

Actually, sometimes these dreams are too exciting and threatening, and I have to wake up just to get away from whatever it is that is after me. For a while indeed, I had a recurring dream that was almost unbearable. It was about the person I had killed, a murder for which I was about to be brought to justice. About four times a year I would dream vividly of this murder, and my impending arrest, and even when I woke up I would not feel safe because I knew that I really had murdered someone in real life, and their name was... was... It was always on the tip of my tongue.

Even now, deep down, I feel there is someone I have killed and that one day it will all come home to roost, but for the life of me I cannot remember who it was. I know they fully deserved it, otherwise I would not have done it, but that is not going to be much of a defence in a murder trial.

I have not had the murder dream for quite a while now, but recently, in the last week, I have started having a different kind of dream, in which people say things which I can remember word for word afterwards. Real dream dialogue. In one of them someone said to me, pointing to an old lady, 'It's amazing that she can still do the twist at the age of 77'. I don't know who the people were, or why I dreamt it, only that that's what one said about the other.

In another, I read a sign outside our nearest post office, in the village of Freshford, which said: 'Closing on 20th Nov.' Now, the shop and post office is under threat of closure, and my wife and I have just been to a fundraising dinner to stave it off – why the exact date, though?

But the third one is the one that made me blink, because it seemed that my dream was trying to write a funny piece for me. It was about the painter Beryl Cook.

Apparently her supporters are scandalised that not one of her paintings has been bought by Tate Modern. It buys all this conceptual rubbish, they say, and doesn't have space for even one canvas by a genuinely popular painter like Beryl Cook.

I do sometimes have sheer action drama dreams. Really exciting James Bond-type ones

In my dream, Nicholas Serota – head of Tate Modern – becomes very worried because he is under constant attack for not admitting anything by Beryl Cook into his kingdom. He still does not want to have any Beryl Cook paintings on his premises, because he has nailed his colours firmly to the mast of conceptual painting, and thinks that Tracey Emin and Damien Hirst are the dog's bollocks (even though neither of them, surprisingly, has yet utilised dogs' bollocks in their conceptual art pieces), but he is worried that the Beryl Cook supporters may plan their revenge.

In particular, he becomes convinced that there is a plot afoot to smuggle Beryl Cook herself inside the Tate Modern and have her die on the premises at the age of eighty, thus promoting a grand scandal. You could see the headlines: 'Painter Banned by Tate Modern Gets Her Revenge!', 'They Could Bar Her Paintings – But They Couldn't Stop Her Final Act!'

So (in my dream) Nicholas Serota circulates photographs of Beryl Cook to all the staff at the Tate Modern, making them memorise her features, and instructing them that if she ever tries to enter she must be thrown out immediately, before she can make her dying gesture on the premises.

I wish I knew what happened next. But that's as far as I dreamt.

I have never met Nicholas Serota.

I am not sure what he looks like, though I always imagine him as one of those John Birt/Alistair Darling/Chris Patten white-haired look-alikes. Actually, I don't know what Beryl Cook looks like either. But the great thing about dreams is that you can dream about famous people even if you don't know what they look like. And now, it seems, dreams can even come up with funny ideas. I hope they get to the punchline next time.

'It doesn't have to be this way, Harry – we could attend couples counselling'

Modern life

What is...
A personal image consultant?

'I just think you might have more sex appeal if you were more of a bastard, Graham'

IN THIS world of media-driven, celebrity-obsessed culture, it seems that 'image' is an all-important concept. It is well-known that politicians and celebrities employ image consultants (often called 'press officers' or 'communications chiefs') to help win over public opinion: think Alastair Campbell, Carole Caplin or Madonna's over-worked press officer who must believe that if there are enough photographs of Madonna on a horse, wearing tweed and a flat cap, then the British public will eventually think she is the archetypal Englishwoman.

With the massive success of image changes and re-vamps in the public eye (please refer to some of the most recent success stories: David Cameron/Prince Charles/Paris Hilton), there was an increasing demand for this sort of service for any old Tom, Dick or Harry. And thus was born the 'personal image consultant': a bit like a life coach for your appearance. If you feel your clothes aren't quite up to scratch, or you have no idea what to wear or how to wear it, you too can call on the services of an image consultant to guide and instruct you.

The general line from the Federation of Image Consultants (TFIC) – based, not in London or Paris or New York, but, amusingly, in that Alan Partridge land of Norwich – reads like a Colemanballs. Image consultants are also called 'personal image developers' – which is a bit like calling a shelf stacker in Sainsbury's a 'stock replenisher', or the people who make sandwiches in the American food-chain, Subway, 'sandwich artists'. The word 'image' is itself often replaced with 'non-verbal communication': a press release from the Federation states, 'People from all professional arenas are increasingly seeking advice on their non-verbal communication skills.' I wonder about my non-verbal communication skills just as much as I wonder about which default salutation I should use on my bounceback.

All the literature is full of this kind of corporate, marketing (mostly American) jargon. When I enquire as to what exactly

> **I wonder about my non-verbal communication skills just as much as I wonder about which default salutation I should use on my bouncebank**

the service can give me, I am told that image consultants can provide 'a variety of services to both individual and corporate clients. This includes personal impact management, total image review, wardrobe management and personal shopping.' Personal impact management? Yes, managing the impact you personally have on someone else. Of course.

The FIC can help you to find an image consultant in your area specifically tailored to your needs. Let's take one consultant: Deborah Gray. Particular areas of focus include colour analysis, style and wardrobe, a 'wardrobe audit' and personal shopping. You can also get something called a 'total image profile', which includes both the colour analysis

and the style and wardrobe consultancy.

And Frances Bodington, currently the president of the Federation of Image Consultants, can provide personal consultations for men and women, 'individual personal branding coaching' and corporate training programmes. A personal image consultation with Frances costs £250 for a half day; a colour analysis costs £175 for two hours; and the 'total image package', consisting of colour analysis, style assessment, a wardrobe audit and a 'style aide memoire' (whatever that is), costs £375. A fairly pricey service – but, as the website states: 'Can you afford not to?'

Image can go a long way these days, but the world of personal image consulting seems to me like a terrible preying on the vulnerable and insecure; a feeding off of the inadequacies of others for personal gain. And the market is endless: the fact is, there will always be people who feel unsure enough about their appearance to search for reassurance. There is even a ghastly TV series called *What Not To Wear*, featuring Trinny and Susannah: two bossy, middle-aged women who have made a living from patronising those who haven't had the time or money (or both) to make sure their wardrobes are up-to-date and flattering, and who 'advise' you on how to 'maximise' your shape with your clothes.

A private image consultation could be a confidence boost for the insecure. But it will probably be the most expensive, jargon-riddled confidence boost you have ever had.

SONALI CHAPMAN

Olden life

Who was...
Cynthia
Plaster Caster?

Left: Cynthia Plaster Caster and her 'algenator' Below: Ian Whitcomb in 1965; the one that got away

DURING THE Swinging Sixties (which actually began in 1965 with the conquest of the American pop charts by the British Invaders spearheaded by Mick Jagger), there gradually appeared in teen fan magazines photos of male rock stars in extremely tight trousers – so tight you could distinguish the amount of small change in their pockets. Freed from the restrictions of the buttoned-up 1950s, it was a coming out party for the hitherto despised and concealed John Thomas.

Attracted to such sights, especially when enhanced by bunched-up haberdashery stuck down the trouser front, some Chicago girls from within the larger consortium of 'groupies' (intense followers of rock groups), turned their avocation into an art form. Led by Cynthia, who as a schoolgirl had been instructed by her teacher to fashion a plaster cast of an object that could retain its shape, and returned with one made from the engorged member of a prominent teen idol, the girls christened themselves The United Plaster Casters Of Chicago.

For their fieldwork (backstage, in hotel rooms, or even at airports) they carried calling cards promising 'Lifelike Models Of Hampton Wicks' and a suitcased kit consisting of wax, clay, some oatmeal perhaps, and aluminium foil, together with an 'algenator' – a receptacle for 'dick dipping'. Cynthia, the chief modeller, was assisted by 'platers' whose job it was to titillate the chosen member into a state of readiness.

This procedure could be dodgy, for an algenator can be cold and the wrong mixture could result in a crumbly mess of ill-starred pastry. Cynthia's detailed notebooks reveal failures such as the attempt to capture Eric Burdon (The Animals) in an aeroplane lavatory during take-off, and Noel Redding (The Jimi Hendrix Experience). The latter was later presented, at his Irish estate, with his failed cast – a pathetic curling white dog's mess of an artwork – shortly before his untimely death. He seemed genuinely pleased.

Redding's bandleader, Jimi Hendrix, is today recognized as Cynthia's greatest success: his cast, which now sits on a plinth in her gallery and is brandished aloft like a holy relic at Caster gatherings, is Olympian in tallness and thickness. Some critics believe it is his real legacy, others regret the lack of colour – for apparently, Mr Hendrix's dong resembled a massive red Yule log richly entwined in blue ivy.

In their heyday, the Plaster Casters were castigated by feminists for being 'in service' to the 'masculine principle'. But today they are championed by as high a social commentator as Camille Paglia, who considers Cynthia and her platers as an example of women taking control – 'A major star being manipulated as if he were in hospital being attended by nurses!'

As one of the British Invaders of 1965 (with my orgasmic breathing hit, 'You Turn Me On'), I had always regretted that I had not been approached by the Casters. At 63, with the Swinging Years long gone, I was thus surprised and thrilled to learn that these brave artists were still at work – and that they needed me.

In an email exchange, Cynthia said she had been 'blown away' by the knowledge that I was still around when so many of her stars were in their graves. 'You were the one I always wanted to cast but could never reach, you were the cutie who'd sent a million hearts fluttering, you must agree to a modelling session and thus become one of my immortal babies!'

Surely I'm over the hill? I protested. No, no, she said, a Hampton never ages! But what about the chill factor? I replied. And the crumble problem? No, no, she said, I have heated gloves and a new paste formula. I must admit my Hampton had started pricking. I hadn't felt this lively since the heady 1960s.

She ended our correspondence by saying: 'It's never too late.'

'Oh, yes it is!' added my wife. And there my case rests.

IAN WHITCOMB

EXPAT
DAVID O'CLEE

Spain

'YOU SEE, the problem with your Spaniard is...' 'What your Spaniard doesn't realise is...' 'Though your Spaniard is basically a lovable guy...' 'But fair do's, show your Spaniard a mountain and he'll build a road through it – and it'll be a bloody good road!'

This is how the 'I've-been-around-Spain-a-bit' Brit talks to a newcomer Brit. It's a formula – one or two hints about Spanish people not understanding the basic facts of modern life, followed by a silly compliment to them about something relatively trivial. But the road-building bit is an improvement on the 'But your Spaniard makes a damn fine waiter!' which is what they used to say. The implication, of course, always has been that we Brits know what we're doing and the poor old Spaniards don't.

I've only been in Spain permanently for a few months but I've been a regular visitor – as a tourist and on business – for a long time. I've never tried either to avoid or seek out other Brits but, whatever happens, I know I'm always going to get a lot of 'helpful' advice from fellow countrymen on how to live my life over here. When I came to Madrid in the early Seventies, I was never lonely.

I'd find myself in really odd places. Probably the oddest was the British Club in Madrid at the bottom of the Gran Via. In this traditional Gentlemen's Club various old buzzards, who saw themselves as the school prefects of the Brit community, got their hands on as many British visitors as they could. Every Friday – even swelteringly hot Fridays in midsummer – they held their traditional roast beef and Yorkshire pudding lunches. Regular members and many Brit visitors invited their Spanish contacts, in the hope that a little of this British culture – along with a dose of non-cultural indigestion – would rub off.

The funniest British Club Brits were people who weren't really British at all. They were a group of short men with heavy accents whose comments about the Spanish were just plain insulting. 'Your

Spaniard' to them was a vicious, cheating, lazy animal with no sense of honour, and with whom these particular 'Brits' had no interest in doing business. They were extreme in their Britishness – insisting on drinking warm English bitter on a baking hot day – and almost muscular in their use of the English vernacular ('It is arraigning cat and dog in the old country'), or complicated mispronunciations like 'Sunday chewings' for 'sand dunes'. They were, of course, Gibraltarians.

Also worth a mention in those days was the curious brigade of whiskery middle-aged English matrons in floral dresses from the British Council. They loved 'educating' the Spanish and invited them for 'tea and Shakespeare' or 'British embroidery in the 19th century' exhibitions. And if you were a really lucky Spaniard, you might get invited to the British Council to drink medium dry sherry with pieces of cheddar cheese on sticks – strictly from 6pm to 8pm. Such a shame that most Spaniards couldn't accept because of their working hours.

And then, at the end of the Seventies, we bought a flat on the edge of a new golf course in Andalucia. Here it wasn't only 'What your Spaniard doesn't understand...' It was also: 'What Harold Wilson and his cronies don't understand...' This is another characteristic of the well-entrenched Brit. He sees himself as a pioneer, a new frontiersman, someone who has fought so many battles, tamed so many natives, and now his mind turns nostalgically to the old country which, because it has been without his advice and consideration for so long, has also become a foreign country.

As time goes by, British opinions on 'Your Spaniard' don't change much – only the type of Brit who expresses them. And there's the pity. Oh for the days when they were patronised by the crisp and fruity voice of a British man of standing. It's much more difficult to patronise people convincingly when you've got suspect vowel sounds.

Mabel is that you? Let me feel your beard.

RANT

JEREMY LEWIS
finds his patience is being stretched...

I WAS WALKING into Richmond Park the other day when I came across a man writhing in apparent agony on the pavement, just by the public lavatories. He was wearing a mauve and black Lycra bicycling kit, his bike was propped against the railings, and his helmet lay on the ground beside him. For a moment I assumed that he had been knocked off his bike, or had suffered a seizure of some kind, and I was about to hurry forward and offer a helping hand when I noticed that, far from showing any concern, my fellow-walkers were either stepping over him or, like bad Samaritans, crossing onto the other side.

It was then I realised that he was not in distress, he was doing stretching exercises, flexing his knees and pointing his toes at the sky like a ballet dancer.

It was a repellent sight, and if I weren't so timid and well-behaved I would have told him to get a grip on himself and refrain from clogging up a public highway.

Joggers and bicyclists of the Lycra variety are familiar hazards when walking in Richmond Park, and very annoying they tend to be: not only do they send walkers scurrying for safety, but – having read some rubbish about how we need to drink so many litres of water a day – they insist on carrying water in plastic bottles which they then hurl into the bracken when no longer needed. But it's when they start stretching that they become intolerable. Invariably, they choose the most public place in which to lean against a tree, flexing slowly up and down or cocking one leg behind them, the ankle grasped in one hand.

There's something horribly smug and narcissistic about it all, and I wish they'd keep it to themselves. When I want to pee in the park I nip behind a bush; they should do the same when overcome by the urge to flex.

ANORAK

KEVIN BERESFORD

THERE IS NOTHING more expressive than the roundabout. With their infinite variety, colour and creativeness, these bitumen beauties lift our sagging spirits on tiresome journeys. The roundabout is truly an oasis on a sea of asphalt.

My interest in roundabouts started on the run-up to Christmas 2002 at my printing company in Redditch, Worcestershire. Wondering what kind of calendar to give out to our clients, we racked our brains and came up with: 'The Roundabouts of Redditch' – twelve stunning photographs of the best traffic islands Worcestershire had to offer.

Redditch is a town famous for needles and fish hooks: it doesn't have a cinema, but it does have three prisons and a 24-hour Tesco, and it also happens to be the home to 42 splendid roundabouts.

We sold over 40,000 calendars and I went on to write a book, *Roundabouts of Great Britain*. I found that I had become hooked on 'bouts. Not only that, it turned out that there were many others like me. All of a sudden roundabout anoraks were coming out of the woodwork. One morning I did an interview about the book for BBC Radio Scotland. Afterwards, a very emotional long-distance truck driver telephoned to say he'd heard my interview and was overjoyed to learn that someone else shared his flaming passion. Apparently he had been a dedicated spotter for years, collecting over time a huge collection of photographs and data on traffic islands and gyratory systems. However, he had kept his hobby a complete secret for fear of ridicule. Upon hearing me he felt he could now bring his secret out in the open and practise his passion in public – and even tell the wife.

If you're interested in roundabout spotting yourself, you might find the following roundabout jargon useful: **'Bouts** – abbreviation of roundabouts; **Chevy** – a roundabout with inclined chevron brickwork; **Crusoe** an extremely large and lush island, mainly un-inhabited; **Desert island** – a boring island; **PMT** – Painted Mini Traffic-island; **Toker** – grass only roundabout; **A Titchmarsh** – a roundabout with flowers in full bloom.

Armed with your jargon, a camera and a flask of tea, it's now time to venture out. If your local islands are hard to locate, try the airport – you will be guaranteed 100 per cent success. (A word of warning, don't try out your new hobby at an airport in Greece – they don't understand the concept of roundabout spotting.) Crematoria also never disappoint – for some reason they always build a 'bout in those places. However, always show respect and proceed quietly. Seek out supermarket retail parks. You will mainly find PMTs but, what the hell, they all count.

Once you have captured all your local 'bouts it might be time to spread your wings and allow yourself to be drawn to the Mecca for roundabouts: Milton Keynes. Your task is made particularly easy by the town's grid system. Or why not try out the Magic Roundabouts of Hemel Hempstead, High Wycombe, Denham, York and Colchester? Or perhaps Swindon's Magic Roundabout in Wiltshire? This is made up of one large 'mother' 'bout at the centre and five small satellite PMTs in orbit around her, so to speak. Traffic circulates in both directions. She's classed as the white knuckle ride of roundabouts... awesome!

Why do we love roundabouts so much? Perhaps it has something to do with us being an island race...

• Kevin Beresford is the author of *Roundabouts of Great Britain* and the President of the United Kingdom Roundabout Appreciation Society.

A beaut of a 'bout

'Should we say something?'

FOUR

Me and my dog

DECCA AITKENHEAD *lost her heart to a snobbish, racist Jamaican goat-chaser*

The great pity of dog ownership is that unless you are very lucky, you have to choose your dog. Whether this involves selection from a pedigree breeder or a moment of weakness in Battersea Dogs Home, the dog has no say in the matter. And so, like a man with a Russian mail-order bride, however loving the relationship you must live forever with the question: would my dog have chosen me?

This is not an affliction of mine, because my dog did choose me. She appeared beside the hammock in the garden within a day of my husband and me arriving in Jamaica. She stayed for about 20 minutes, very much the Victorian lady dropping by to greet new neighbours, and the next day was back with an air of shy friendliness, departing again with the precision of one who would be mortified to outstay a welcome. Her visits lengthened, growing steadily less formal, but she asked for nothing, and when offered refreshments would politely decline. When first invited to step inside the house she hesitated, more as a show of respect for the threshold than from any real doubt, and indoors this little ballet of manners was repeated at each entrance to a new room.

It was an old-fashioned courtship, for she was a dignified lady who did not need an owner; her love had to be earned, and each concession to romance was an elegant equation of trust and surrender. By the time she had acquired a name, Charlotte, a hand-fed diet of lobster and chicken, and a place in our bed, it was a love affair as passionate as any I have ever known, and everlasting. But it was one she chose for herself.

Decca with Charlotte and the puppies

Before we moved into the village Charlotte had been known as Humphrey, and lived at Jake's, a rather barefoot-bijou hotel of beach cottages favoured by creative types from America and Britain. Guests loved Charlotte. Being a wise creature, she chose to spend her time with them, and steered well clear of Jamaicans. Jamaicans do not love dogs. Though even the locals had to concede that there was something rather special about Charlotte after the occasion when she found a litter of orphaned kittens. Carrying them one by one in her mouth back to Jake's, she presented them at the kitchen door, saw that they were fed, and curled around them at night to keep them warm.

But as a hotel pet Charlotte was leading an under-realised life. Guests would pack up after a week or so and kiss her goodbye, never dreaming of what this dog could become, given more than a holiday romance. As Charlotte installed herself in our life, she began to grow.

'Have you got something suitable for kicking after a hard day at the office?'

The car came first. She took a great deal of initial persuading to climb in, and spent her maiden journey up the lane to the post office looking so shocked we weren't sure she cared for it. But she was in love with driving, and from that day on enjoyed nothing more than being chauffeured around Jamaica like a princess. The sight of a dog in a car was as startling to Jamaicans as a pig might look in a Rolls Royce in London.

Charlotte soon became a terrific snob. She liked people to see that she had her own family now, and when visitors came to the house would modify her bark according to a very precise appraisal of their social status. Those she considered riff-raff would get an awful racket. If she was so rude to them that I had to scold her, she would look up ruefully and laugh, as if to say, 'I know they're your friends, but really, come on.'

Charlotte became such a snob that even her own puppies were beneath her. She was mortified when she came on heat, embarrassed by the indignity of it all, and when her puppies were born it was all we could do to get her to bother even feeding them. The poor little things cramped her style, and as one by one we found them homes she looked delighted to be shot of them.

As time passed, her memory of life at Jake's faded away. She became a great enthusiast for new routines. At dawn she would be up first, eyeing the running shoes and giving the impression that if she wore a watch she would be glancing at it. The morning run was a source of unending joy to Charlotte, starting with the warm-up stretch. Positioning herself beside me, she would study my stretches and try to copy them, extending out her paws and glancing over to check that she had the move exactly right. But the real highlight of the run was the goat-chasing opportunities that lay in the fields behind the bay. She quickly clocked which areas lay in view of the farmer's house, and would trot past grazing goats as if she couldn't be less interested – but once round the corner, she was off like a greyhound, taking great gleeful bounds

Charlotte became such a snob that even her own puppies were beneath her. The poor little things cramped her style

across the grass. She never bothered to bite them, but would stretch her neck forward and nudge the stragglers along.

There was one trait learned at Jake's which Charlotte never lost, and I'm afraid to say it was racism. Our dog is indelibly racist. Years of experience had taught her that white people were guests, the ones who liked to pet and feed her, so were all right. Black people were more likely to shout at her, so were not. Her racism was so highly developed that she could tell the difference between mixed race and a deep tan at 20 paces, and nothing we ever did could stop her treating the former to a throaty growl.

I have not experienced anything more devastating than leaving Charlotte behind. She never knew that we would one day move back to London, and we had no way of telling her. She trusted us, and we broke her trust, and it is more than I can bear. But a quarantine kennel for six months is something we could not do to our beautiful, free dog. And so we lobby the Jamaican government to change its rabies vaccination laws, and we think about smuggling her home on a yacht – and every few months we go back to Jamaica to be with her again.

The drive over the mountains from Montego Airport to Jake's is winding and tortuously long. By the time we arrive the cottages are in darkness, the hotel asleep. As we pick our way down to the beach we can scarcely breathe, so suffocated are we by excitement, and by the sand we pause and whistle her special whistle into the hot night air. For a moment we wait. And then there she is, a honey streak of gold flying towards us, spinning circles of amazement and joy as she throws herself at our feet.

None of us can sleep the first night. When dawn comes, and the reunion's first tearful delirium is beginning to settle, she sidles over to the suitcase to look for the running shoes. The goat-chasing that morning is accompanied by a particular victory whoop in her tail, and when afterwards we sit down by the pool for breakfast, her very favourite moment arrives. Whichever guests Charlotte has currently been flirting with appear for coffee and spot her. 'Humphrey!' they coo, approaching to pet her. 'Good morning, Humph.'

And she stares for a second, with utter disdain, as though she has never seen these people before in her life. Then she turns her back, slinks under my chair, and nudges me for a stroke. As I blush and pat her head, she may throw them one final, cutting glance – just to be sure that they see she has her family back now.

'And this is our lack-of-water feature'

We got it licked!

DAVID HORRY *exclusively reveals some of the bizarre, unissued stamps collected by his grandfather, Hedley Adams Mobbs*

Hedley Adams Mobbs and King George V had, between them, the two finest collections of unissued stamps in the world. The King had built up one of the greatest stamp collections of all time. Hedley Mobbs, my maternal grandfather, specialised in the stamps that fell by the philatelic wayside.

It was the King who first involved Hedley Mobbs in philately. In 1926, around the time of the General Strike, he was summoned to Windsor Castle by His Majesty. Hedley Mobbs at that time had put together a marvellous collection of unissued Penny Blacks which he had built up from a small collection given to his grandfather, Adam Adams, by William Ewart Gladstone.

Hedley Mobbs was asked by the King and Sir Ewerby Thorpe, Keeper of the King's Philately, to maintain the unissued items from the Royal Philatelic Collection. These unissued items were a possible source of embarrassment to His Majesty because of their interesting subject matters.

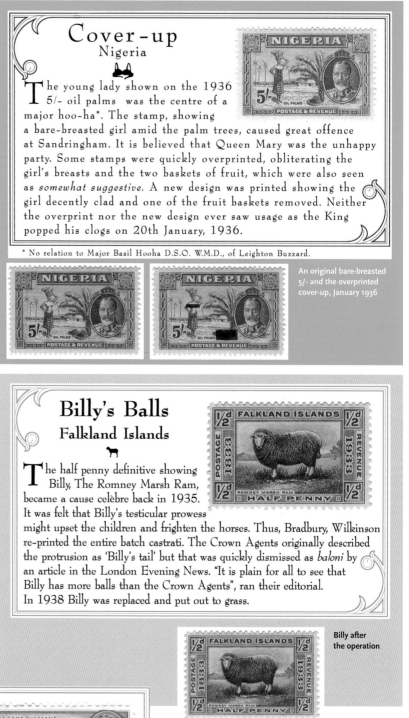

Cover-up
Nigeria

The young lady shown on the 1936 5/- oil palms was the centre of a major hoo-ha*. The stamp, showing a bare-breasted girl amid the palm trees, caused great offence at Sandringham. It is believed that Queen Mary was the unhappy party. Some stamps were quickly overprinted, obliterating the girl's breasts and the two baskets of fruit, which were also seen as *somewhat suggestive*. A new design was printed showing the girl decently clad and one of the fruit baskets removed. Neither the overprint nor the new design ever saw usage as the King popped his clogs on 20th January, 1936.

* No relation to Major Basil Hooha D.S.O. W.M.D., of Leighton Buzzard.

An original bare-breasted 5/- and the overprinted cover-up, January 1936

Billy's Balls
Falkland Islands

The half penny definitive showing Billy, The Romney Marsh Ram, became a cause celèbre back in 1935. It was felt that Billy's testicular prowess might upset the children and frighten the horses. Thus, Bradbury, Wilkinson re-printed the entire batch castrati. The Crown Agents originally described the protrusion as 'Billy's tail' but that was quickly dismissed as *baloni* by an article in the London Evening News. "It is plain for all to see that Billy has more balls than the Crown Agents", ran their editorial. In 1938 Billy was replaced and put out to grass.

Billy after the operation

Pheasant
Great Britain

King George V cared for little in life except for shooting and philately. John Betjeman's *Continental Dew* (1937) *"Death of King George V"* sums it up prettywell:-   Spirits of well-shot woodcock, partridge, snipe
Flutter and bear him up the Norfolk sky:
In that red house in a red mahogany book-case
The stamp collection waits with mounts long dry.
In more common parlance *"if 'e couldn't stick 'em in a stamp album 'e'd bloody shoot 'em!"* This glorious design from Bradbury, Wilkinson was due for release 12th August 1936. However, KGV had already gone to the great shooting-party in the sky.

Thorpe knew that Hedley Mobbs was a man of unquestionable integrity who would maintain the collection and its secrets. This explains the depth of the Mobbs collection as it was being supplied by the King himself.

In total, Hedley Mobbs was Keeper of the Royal Unissued Stamps for almost 35 years.

What you see here is just a small selection from his collection.

Stamps shown were taken from Horry's book, The Unissued Stamps of King George V, *published by Murray Payne. His previous book* The Unissued Stamps of King George VI *is also available from Murray Payne*

Last respects

*When trying to arrange her mother's funeral, **ANGELA HUTH** found the Church of England somewhat lacking in tact*

The arranging of a funeral is never an agreeable experience: it's made much worse when the organiser is confronted with disillusion.

A few months ago my mother died. My sister and I set about all the complicated palaver that follows a death. The meeting with the undertaker was fine. He was a dignified and tactful man, concerned only to do things in the way we wished. His was a small, rural family firm. In such businesses, I have learned, funeral matters are conducted with sympathetic efficiency. They don't go in for the pained looks and soppy voices that some of the bigger, more commercial firms deem necessary.

Then we met the vicar. The fact that it was a woman vicar was unnerving; my mother, well into her nineties, was allergic to such people. We feared some protest from within her coffin, but there was nothing much we could do.

The vicar, let us call her Denise, came jauntily into the room. She had crystallised blonde hair shot with pink tufts, glinting lipstick, a dog collar and jeans. I sensed at once that she and I might not see eye to eye, but kept my cool.

She began in that professionally concerned voice, adopted by social workers, that makes my hackles rise – but then I admit I have particularly sensitive hackles where the modernised Church of England is concerned. She began to 'talk through' the order of service, listing what we wanted. After some ten minutes I ventured to say the thing I really wanted, and really minded about, were the official words employed. It had to be the 1662 *Book of Common Prayer*, I said, or else... At that moment I could think of no appropriate threat.

'There is no provision,' said Denise, looking as astounded as if I'd requested terrorists to sing in the choir. Her extraordinary response caused my hackles to rise so violently I failed to ask the obvious question: do you not have a *Book of Common Prayer*?

Denise went on to explain that she, too, had been brought up with 1662, but had come to appreciate the latest version of the prayer book. 'It's respectful,' she said.

'Respectful it may be,' I said, 'but it's not beautiful.' She nodded. 'So why can't we have respectful and beautiful, which is what we want?'

There followed a few of those usual points in old v. new arguments that score poorly:

'So why does no one translate Shakespeare into modern English?' I lob. 'He's far harder than the *Bible*.'

The fact it was a woman vicar was unnerving; my mother, well into her nineties, was allergic to such people

No comment. We move on. I sensed everyone was simmering. Finally, she made a request. 'I want to chat about Mum,' she said.

Why did she want to talk about her mother? It turned out she didn't. It was our mother she wanted to discuss: could we supply a few telling adjectives? It seemed she was bent on giving a sermon about a woman she had never met, even though several members of the family were going to pay tribute, and everyone in the congregation would have known our mother well.

Why did Denise, a keen supporter of respectful language, not see that to refer to our mother as 'Mum' was the height of disrespect? It was impertinent, patronising, infuriating. Don't vicars have lessons in diplomacy these days? Can they not distinguish between those who enjoy cosy chumminess, and those who prefer gruff, dignified talk at moments of adversity?

With the end of the meeting came a feeling of terrible failure on my part. It looked as though my mother wouldn't be getting what she wanted, and nor would we. I was determined to try harder from that moment on.

So the next day I rang a bishop, an archdeacon and a deacon. I learned there is no rule about what services should be used. It's all a matter of negotiation with the vicar. The deacon himself had given a 1662 funeral only the week before.

Armed with this vital knowledge, I turned to my sister, who was more likely to keep her cool when trying to re-persuade Denise to do what we wanted. When she described my research among Church toffs, Denise remarked, 'Ooh, she must have minded a lot.' – She did, Denise, she did.

My tactful sister also managed to persuade Denise not to give a sermon about a woman she had never met, but to reflect instead on death and God.

In the end, we got what we wanted but, in the heightened state that comes after a death, at some cost. You'd think people would be allowed to have the service of their liking with no fuss. But no: one of the Church of England's blind follies is to try to regiment its diminishing congregations, herd us all into the same mould, serve us up with council pamphlet language, and extinguish all mystery. No wonder those of us who loved the old Church, its language and formality, its inspiring sense of having to aspire, are abandoning it in ever-increasing numbers and with ever-increasing sadness.

I once met...
Beryl Cook

It was pure serendipity. While working as a theatre critic I went to the Plymouth Arts Centre to see the American stand-up Ray Hassett. While I was waiting for the show to begin I wandered upstairs to the gallery where the director, Bernard Samuels, was hanging some paintings for the next exhibition. I soon became quite fascinated by the paintings, which were full of rough humour.

I recognised the Donald McGill saucy seaside element, but some of them had a touch of malevolence – there was spite as well as wit. Others were entirely joyous: the Duke of Edinburgh swinging the Queen off the ground in a *Come Dancing* jubilee celebration, blank-faced holiday visitors chomping sandwiches, seemingly unaware that the bus shelter where they were sitting was covered in graffiti like 'I need sex', 'Jimmy Carter pees the bed', or 'I shagged a Froggy,' lovingly reproduced in all their rough glory.

Bernard told me that this was the first exhibition of a Plymouth landlady who was so shy that she wasn't even going to her own exhibition. Her name was Beryl Cook, and she ran a boarding-house near the Hoe. I went to see her.

At that time Beryl didn't have much faith in her painting, and relied on the money she got from B&B clients. She told me how she started, painting on driftwood gathered on the beach in Looe, before graduating to hardboard. I arranged for a photographer to take some prints and contacted the *Sunday Times*. The editor of the colour magazine commissioned me to do an interview.

I took Beryl out for a day in Plymouth. We went to the Breton Arms for lunch. As soon as we got in the barman beckoned me to the counter. 'Sorry, sir. Women are not allowed in here at lunchtime.' I was dumbfounded, and sat tight, but Beryl was more pragmatic. 'Let's go to another bar,' she said.

I was disappointed at her failure to protest against this unreasonable treatment of her sex. But Beryl doesn't have a romantic view of women in general. Look at the grotesques in her paintings. Particularly cruel is the depiction of a lumpy lady in standard seduction kit of black underwear, stockings and suspenders: it is called Fantastic Fun Set, and the woman has clearly been sold a promise that is unlikely to be fulfilled.

Later we went to the Arts Centre, where an experimental company was running a show which showed actors having fits of hysteria. 'I do love hysteria,' Beryl said mysteriously.

I later discovered that this very shy lady liked to visit the more raucous clubs and pubs in Plymouth to watch strippers and drag acts, not only recalling the performances in her paintings, but the reactions of the audiences as well.

The piece about her was a great success, and Beryl was launched on a career, becoming in due course the nation's favourite artist. Before Beryl was launched, the staff on the colour magazine wanted to buy some of her paintings, knowing that she was going to be famous. As they had all been painted on hardboard it was a heavy task taking them up on the train and getting them over to their office.

At the end of our association she gave me one of the bus shelter paintings. I had it on my wall for ten years, but after moving house my wife and I decided that it didn't suit our new abode. I took it to a local estate agent who ran a monthly auction. They accepted it with a reserve of £200, but then I got an irate call from the auctioneer.

'You can't expect me to display this!'
'Why not?'
'Have you seen what is written on the walls of the bus shelter?'
'Yes,' I replied. 'It's authentic. She copied it.'
'But – "Nigel is a wanker"!'
'It must have been up there. She goes up to the Hoe early mornings and copies it all down.'
'Strange occupation,' said the auctioneer. 'This is a respectable firm. I think you'd better take it away.'

In the end I took my bus shelter painting to Bonhams, who auctioned it off for £4,500 (so much for the £200 reserve), and my wife and I spent the lot on a cruise down the Danube.

ALLEN SADDLER

RANT

ROGER LEWIS *doesn't like quaint market towns...*

I HATE quaint market towns, cut off from the rest of humanity when Beeching tore up the train tracks. The West Country and the Welsh Marches are full of them. You know the kind of place – the peeling Georgian terraces, the merchants' villas divided into flats for Bulgarian asparagus-pickers on benefits, the shops selling unpalatable jam and novelty scented candles, the smallholders' stalls in the Corn Exchange, where root-faced lesbians or argumentative queers in mail-order wax jackets sell gone-off organic sausages and eggs flecked with authentic chicken ordure.

There's nothing to do in such a town. I end up poking around in the Spastics' Charity Shop trying on dead people's blazers or examining the videos of the second series of *Oh No! It's Selwyn Froggitt*. In the local museum, now called the Heritage Centre, I gaze uncomprehendingly at agricultural implements.

Quaint market towns are a gastronomic black hole. Apart from the chippy, which will usually be named The Cod Father, The Merrie Fryer or Batterlicious, the only halfway-decent places are Balti Towers and Call Me Halal, none of which is open at lunchtime. At The Holly Bush everything comes out of the microwave. The lamb I had was frozen at the centre and covered with ice crystals. The waitress kept saying 'Not a problem!' and when she dropped the butter on the floor she picked it up covered with dog hairs and popped it back on to my plate.

There is always a grander establishment in the Town Square with a Les Routiers plaque. At the bar will be the local auctioneer, an alcoholic proud of his canary-yellow waistcoat. Next to him are burly people with loud, piercing laughs and personal cider tankards and an ancient squadron leader sounding off about golf and chemotherapy.

The pavements are filled with under-age putty-faced girls with snout-studs and plump, ugly toddlers called Kellan or Kallum, Kyle or Keanu.

None of this lot will be missed.

Are you an Oldie? tell-tale signs

We first printed this simple self-diagnosis in 1993. Now we have revised it for newer readers, for those who are still unsure – or simply for those who have forgotten...

1. When you hear of 'Big Brother', do you still think of George Orwell?
2. Do you not only talk to yourself, but see nothing odd about it?
3. Do you know quite a lot of poems by heart?
4. Do you spend more than an average amount of time in stationery shops?
5. Do you refer to 'the wireless'?
6. Do you remember who was 'Awfully worried about Jim'?
7. Are you obsessively concerned about the size and shape of spoons?
8. Do you mend clothes rather than throw them away?

Have you now forgotten where you were when Kennedy was shot?

9. Do you write letters?
10. Do you still wind your watch up?
11. Do you know what a pronoun is?

12. Are there at least 10 people in your address book who are dead?
13. Do you know any prayers apart from the Lord's Prayer?
14. Do you save string?
15. Are you frightened of going to the Barbican?

16. Can you waltz?
17. Do you go around turning lights off?
18. Do you clean your shoes with a brush and proper shoe polish?
19. Have you ever been to a Japanese restaurant?
20. Do you own an iPod?
21. Do you shout at the television or radio?
22. Did you watch *Grumpy Old Men* and think: 'They're not old!'
23. Have you come to hate Christmas?
24. Have you now forgotten where you were when Kennedy was shot?
25. Have you taken out a subscription to *The Oldie*?

If you answered 'Yes' to more than 10 questions (and 'No' to questions 19 and 20), then congratulations! You are most definitely an Oldie.

Behind the catchphrase

ALICE PITMAN *meets veteran actor* **LESLIE PHILLIPS**, *whose colourful and varied seventy-year career has been so much more than a few 'Ding dongs'...*

'This last year has been the busiest of my life. Enjoyably busy, as there is nothing worse than not being busy if you're an actor.'

I am having quite possibly the worst cup of coffee of my life in the bar at Simpson's-in-the-Strand with the remarkable Leslie Phillips, just prior to his appearance at an Oldie lunch.

He takes a sip from his cup and pulls a face. 'Sorry about the coffee,' he murmurs, as though it is his fault.

Leslie Phillips is now 82, though he looks ten years younger. He is nattily be-suited, an added touch of jauntiness provided by a pink comb protruding from his inside jacket pocket. I decide that his well-preserved appearance must be due in part to the fact that his mind has been kept active, for apart from a spell in the army during the war, he has not stopped acting since he took to the stage as a child actor in 1935.

His career has seen him in over a hundred films and two hundred theatrical roles. He has appeared alongside a roll call of stars, from Dame Anna Neagle to John Malkovich and, more recently, Peter O'Toole, in the much-acclaimed film *Venus*. The latter recently garnered him a BIFA for best supporting actor: a far cry from his impoverished working-class Tottenham origins, the third and last child of Frederick (whose work in a filthy gas cooker factory contributed to his premature death at the age of 44) and Cecilia, to whom he dedicated the award. 'I was so surprised to get it I hadn't prepared a speech. When I got up to the microphone, all I could think of was my mother.'

The acceptance speech created quite a stir. After commencing with his trademark lecherous catchphrase 'Hello!', he continued: 'In 1993, at the age of 92...' The audience laughed, anticipating an amusing story. He went on, '...my mother was mugged in the street and killed.

'She would have been very proud of me tonight.' He held up the trophy and walked off to a stunned silence.

'It went from absolute high comedy to tragedy, but life's like that, don't you think?' Leslie says. 'My sister was so shaken by my mother's death she only outlived her by six months. You never get over something like that.'

His mother first introduced an 11-year-old Leslie to the theatre by taking him along to an audition for the Italia Conti Stage School.

He received elocution lessons to rid him of his broad Cockney accent, seen in those days as a major impediment to an aspiring actor. 'All my friends and family were Londoners, real Cockneys – my brother is still a Cockney. They found it hard to recognise the new me, though my voice has without doubt played an enormous part in my success.'

By the age of 14 Leslie was working in West End plays alongside such luminaries as Vivien Leigh, Lilli Palmer (on whom he had a tremendous crush), and Rex Harrison ('something of a role model for me, though I could never have reached anything like his heights in the philandering department').

What was Vivien Leigh like?

'Oh, she was wonderful. She had a special way of saying my name...

'She would draw out the last syllable: "Les-liee, daarling..."' Laurence Olivier would come to the theatre in his Fleet Air Arm uniform. 'He was delightful. I bumped into him again years later when I was acting in *The Cherry Orchard*.

'He would come to the rehearsals, sidle up to me, and say, "Leslie, a few tips..."'

'If I was doing a scene on camera and Peter O'Toole was off, he'd choose that moment to send me up'

During the war, Leslie was commissioned as a second lieutenant in the Durham Light Infantry, but was declared unfit for service just before D-Day. 'I had a nervous illness which caused paralysis.' His pal Johnny Mould took over his platoon, and was one of the first to be killed in France. The burden Leslie felt at being left behind was compounded by the news that his brother had been badly injured in Italy. 'I still feel tremendous guilt, although there was nothing I could do about it. I suppose it was the luckiest thing that ever happened to me.'

After the war he resumed his theatrical career, also becoming a familiar voice on radio with 250 episodes of *The Navy Lark*. His big film break came with *Les Girls* (1957), a Gene Kelly musical.

The three early Carry Ons, followed by the Doctor series of films, established his reputation for playing upper-class silly asses and womanising smoothies.

In *Carry On Nurse* (1959) we first

heard him utter the words, 'Ding dong'. Catchphrases such as 'Lumme' and 'Well, hello' soon followed. 'Even today, I am regularly ding-donged as I walk around London,' he says, seeming both pleased and slightly annoyed.

I wonder if, despite success in more serious roles in the latter half of his career (*Falstaff* at the RSC, *Empire of the Sun*, *Out of Africa*), it bothers him that he will be forever associated with English stereotype comic roles of the 1950s and '60s?

'It did at one time, as it was only a very small part of my career – and we never got any money from them. They exported these films all around the world – *Carry On Nurse* went on to become the biggest grossing British film ever in the US – but not one penny went to the poor bloody actors...'

His private life has been suitably colourful. He married Penelope Bartley in 1948, producing four children. As his career took off, long absences away from home meant they inevitably grew apart. 'I was guilty of neglecting the family a little, but she made no objection to the money coming in...' He began an affair with Caroline Mortimer, stepdaughter of John Mortimer, and Bartley divorced him in 1965. He and Mortimer split after nine years as she wanted children and he didn't. 'I already had all the children I thought I could reasonably handle.'

He kept in contact with Penny Bartley until her death in a fire in 1982. Shortly after, Leslie married Angela Scoular, a former Bond girl, whom he had met while working on a play in 1976.

We discuss his recent autobiography *Hello*, part show-business gossip, part confessional, interspersed with endearing domestic details about much-loved dogs, cats and motorcars. There's also the occasional smattering of sex, the more explicit passages sitting oddly alongside prosaic accounts of films and West End plays.

When I ask him about the famous people he has worked with, Leslie worries that he might come across as a bit of a name-dropper.

Among his favourites were Kay Kendall, Kenneth Williams, Ronnie Barker, Joan Plowright, Denholm Elliott and Terry Thomas.

And those he disliked? Roy Boulting – 'The only

Top: Leslie Phillips and Geraldine McEwan in *For Better, For Worse* at London's Comedy Theatre in 1952
Above: Leslie Phillips and Peter O'Toole in *Venus* (image courtesy Nicola Dove/Eyebox)

man I have ever physically hit' – and Sir Seymour Hicks: 'An overbearing shit.'

What film has he enjoyed working on the most?

'Oh, *Venus*, I think. I'm very proud of that film.'

Was Peter O'Toole fun to work with?

He hesitates. 'I wouldn't say fun. Powerful. He's a great actor, with a very strong personality and a sense of humour. If I was doing a scene on-camera and he was off camera, he'd choose that moment to send me up.'

He hopes *Venus* might open a few doors for him. He'll consider anything as long as it's good: comedy or drama, he doesn't mind.

'I like to play villains best... Bastards,' he says, with a mock-wicked leer. 'I don't look like a villain, you see, so it's quite nice.'

So no plans to retire then?

'I don't consider it a word in my vocabulary.'

THE OLDIE ANNUAL 2008   **21**

Cranley Gardens in 1983.
Murderer Dennis Nilsen
lived on the second floor

Deadly estates

STANLEY PRICE *moved into Cranley Gardens just before murderer Dennis Nilsen was arrested. The move was riddled with strange coincidences involving the gruesome crimes...*

The coincidences began as soon as our offer for the house in Muswell Hill was accepted. I was in the middle of filming the pilot episode of a TV series I had written. The next day I realised our leading actress, Liza Goddard, was under par. In a coffee-break she confided she had just been gazumped for a house she and her husband were desperate to buy. It was perfect for them. She was married to the rock'n'roll star Alvin Stardust, and the house had a huge cellar for a recording studio. Where was the house, I asked? In Muswell Hill, she said. What street? Cranley Gardens, she said. What number? I guessed what the answer would be and was right. I had just bought Mr and Mrs Stardust's dream house. I admitted the buyer was me.

She looked at me as though I was a deadly snake who had just crawled out from under a rock. I protested that I hadn't gazumped her, I had simply offered the asking price. She said she had made a good offer and had been

When I saw Kate Adie in front of our house with a microphone I knew we were in trouble

accepted. Nobody had told me that, I said. In that case the estate agents had screwed them, she said. I felt a slight chill for the rest of the filming.

We moved into the house in late January 1983. It badly needed

redecorating and we called in the two Jimmies, middle-aged Irish cousins who were always cheerful. On their fourth day they arrived less than cheerful.

'Quite a commotion in the street,' the older Jimmy said.

'What sort of commotion?'

'Police, reporters, TV cameras. Didn't you hear the news last night?'

I shook my head. They looked embarrassed and the younger Jimmy passed me his *Daily Mirror*. The headline announced the arrest of one Dennis Nilsen for murdering a large, but as yet unspecified, number of young men in his flat in Cranley Gardens. You may recall that Nilsen was caught because, after strangling his victims, he dismembered them and put them down the main drain. Neighbours downhill of him – we were fortunately three houses up – complained of blocked drains. Dyno-Rod were called out and got a nasty surprise. The police followed.

I went out into the street. It was a great commotion of police cars with flashing lights, television cameras, reporters and bug-eyed spectators. When I saw Kate Adie in front of our house with a hand-mike I knew we were in real trouble. In those days she only did serious civil wars, major catastrophes and atrocities. Later that week I saw police digging in the wasteland behind our houses. Tourist coaches were now parking outside our house to disembark ghouls with cameras to take their souvenir pictures of the slaughterhouse. Meanwhile, Nilsen was confessing freely and, to our dismay, our street hogged the headlines for weeks. He had killed up to six young men in his 18 months in his Cranley Gardens flat and probably about nine in his previous flat in Melrose Avenue, Cricklewood. Forensics were working overtime to establish the exact number.

My wife Judy's and my initial reaction was to want out. Our new home had been poisoned. We would pay off the Jimmies, sell the house and go and live as far away from Muswell Hill as we could – South America, South London even. But who, I asked, would now buy the house given its grisly locale? Judy had a brainwave – the Alvin Stardusts. If he really wanted that recording studio in the basement desperately enough...

'No one could be that desperate,' I said.

'Just try,' she said. 'We could bring the price down a bit.'

'We might have to give it away.'

But I did phone. Liza answered the phone and was affable. After a few pleasantries I said, 'You've probably heard what's happened in Cranley Gardens.'

'How could one not?' Did I detect schadenfreude in her voice?

'My wife's been very upset by it all. More sensitive soul that I am, but I was just wondering...'

Liza didn't even wait for her cue, 'The answer's no. No way.' And that really ended the conversation.

A week or so later I went to a Writers' Guild function at the Purcell Room on the South Bank. I found myself talking to Bill Craig, a popular Scots TV-writer, and novelist Fay Weldon. I told them of my recent move to Cranley Gardens. They both went a little pale,

Dennis Nilsen

It took years for people to forget that Cranley Gardens had been home to Britain's record-holding serial killer

but I was getting used to that. Bill Craig interrupted me: 'That's bloody incredible. I live in Cricklewood – Melrose Avenue, where he did the other half-dozen or so. I was probably putting out my garbage bags next to his – with the bits in them.'

Fay Weldon now looked even paler. 'Three weeks ago my daughter went to the Job Centre in Kentish Town. That's where he worked. She was interviewed by him.' There was a silence. We couldn't decide what the odds were against a coincidence like that, but we did agree he wouldn't have been caught, or at least not so quickly, if he'd had a car. With a car you can bundle the body into the boot and drive it out to Rickmansworth reservoir or the lea near Bishop's Stortford – well, we were all writers. Without a car the problem of corpse-disposal is tricky and very messy.

For a while, to avoid morbid questioning, I didn't tell people where I lived. The other residents in the

street were equally traumatised. Some petitioned Haringey Council to destroy the house and rename the street, as had happened to Christie's house in Rillington Place, Notting Hill. The council turned down the suggestion. Instead some developers bought the house for a knockdown price and refurbished the flats. The estate agent involved advertised them emphasising the Nilsen connection as a selling point. The advertisement was withdrawn after local objections to the Estate Agents' Association. The flats were sold without difficulty, but at under the going rate. Inevitably the couple who bought Nilsen's actual flat were interviewed by the local paper and seemed to like the idea of living in a famous flat.

At the Old Bailey, Nilsen, 38 at the time, was found guilty on six counts of murder and two of attempted murder, though he had actually murdered over 15.

It took some years for people to forget that Cranley Gardens had been the home to Britain's record-holding serial killer, but eventually house prices soared in line with everywhere else.

My TV pilot was made but never became a series. We stayed on in our house for another 17 years. Nilsen is now in the 24th year of his life sentence. Alvin Stardust still tours his rock'n'roll show and lives up north. Liza Goddard lives in Norfolk with another husband. Kate Adie has written her autobiography and doesn't mention Cranley Gardens.

'Are you ready to be thrown out yet, Sir?'

Homework time

ZENGA LONGMORE *thinks her daughter's homework may be a form of divine retribution...*

Have you ever wondered where the expression 'God pays his debts without money' comes from? Neither have I. I'm not even sure what it means.

However, whenever my 15-year-old daughter, Omalara, hands me her homework with the order, 'It should have been in last Monday, so get cracking,' I feel, in some obscure way, that I am re-paying God's moneyless debts.

During my halcyon schooldays, my eldest brother, Roy, was the official 'homeworker' of our household. With great groans and murmurings, he would dutifully plough through Graham Greene, Anthony Trollope and dense swathes of Hemingway. With three sisters and two brothers to do homework for, Roy had little else to occupy his time but churn out school dissertations.

'What's the essay supposed to be about?' he would sigh.

'I can't remember.'

'Well, how long should it be?'

'Sort of essay length, I suppose.

Anyway, just have it done by tomorrow.' And with that, I would settle back to a carefree evening of watching *The Avengers* or *The Prisoner* without sparing a thought for the hapless Roy, trapped in a room grappling with George Eliot.

Although newspaper columnists lament that comprehensive schools are getting worse, the bald facts are that little has changed during the last 30 years. Older siblings and parents still sweat over homework which seldom gets marked by the teacher. A doting dad recently told me that his daughter will pass all her A levels even if she fails her exams because she has received such good marks for reams of coursework he has written for her.

When my daughter reached school age I commenced on the repayment of my previously mentioned debts (homework starts at four years old these days). In true Greek tragedian style, retribution followed sin. Roy is still around, but refuses to read unwholesome authors for

his nephews and nieces, claiming that a lifetime of homeworking for himself and his siblings has irreparably addled his brain. A brain which, as he sometimes reminds me, was never too far from being addled to begin with.

Omalara discovered that homework was not for her at the age of six. Her teacher, disabled by the national curriculum, had careered wildly from the Victorians to the Greeks, back to the Vikings and finally skidded with a crash at the Tudors. All in the space of a term.

'Were the Victorians from Victoria?' she asked one evening, as she pondered over her primary school history sheet.

'No, Victoria was the name of the Queen at that time.'

'So was there a Queen called Greek?'

'No, the Greeks came from Greece.'

'So the Tudors come from Tudoreece?'

'No, the surname of the Kings and Queens was Tudor.'

'So who came from Viking? Or was their surname Viking?'

'The Vikings came from Scandinavia, and they were called things like Eric and Canute.'

'Eric and what? Oh my days!'

With a pitiful whimper, Omalara decided the whole idea of schoolwork, homework and history was beyond human comprehension. But it doesn't seem to have done her any harm. The harm has been done to me. From then on, a ghastly routine was set; the routine of demanding, 'You do my homework while I watch telly.'

Writing Omalara's English homework is a sickeningly pride-wounding task. My deathless prose is never marked above a C minus and is invariably accompanied by hurtful comments such as 'Appalling punctuation, and tenses, Omalara, tenses!'

At dead of night, when good Christian folk should be sunk in swinish slumber, I am likely to be discovered straining both mind and soul over Arthur Miller, Alice Walker or Wilkie Collins. Recently, the last vestiges of my sanity were very nearly destroyed by a five-page essay on Harold Pinter's *The Birthday Party*: 'Discuss the dimensional tragicomic factors relating to the protagonist's intrinsic breakdown of communication.' I didn't go as far as reading the actual play – after all, there are limits to human endurance – but I looked up readers' comments on the internet and proceeded to cobble together a two thousand-word essay. I spent all Sunday labouring over it and fussed over it on Monday. On Tuesday I re-polished

Narcissus receives a Valentine

it. Then I gazed at it in amazement. I had produced a work of genius; one of those powerful, yet effortless pieces of literature which few modern essayists are able to rustle up. Charles Lamb, had he composed it, would have smirked with self-satisfaction. I lovingly eased it into an envelope and handed it to Omalara with instructions not to smudge or crease it. I was vaguely concerned that its brilliance would

At dead of night, I am likely to be discovered straining mind and soul over Arthur Miller and Alice Walker

reach the attention of Melvyn Bragg, who would invite Omalara to his BBC studios for an in-depth discussion on her searing critical analysis of *The Birthday Party*. Perhaps Harold Pinter himself would be invited. Would an intrinsic tragicomic situation arise? Omalara's

only escape route would be to reply to tricky questions in Pinterese:

Melvyn: 'What do you think of Pinter's dimensional factors?'

Omalara: 'There's something ticking in my room.'

Well, something like that, anyway.

A week later Omalara returned home with an envelope marked 'English'.

'It's the essay, it's the essay!' I chirped with the excitement of a novelist about to read his first review. 'What marks did I get for Harold Pinter?'

'What Harold Pinter?'

'The Harold Pinter that took me three days to complete.'

'Oh, that. The Harold Pinter teacher left last week. He's gone to run a creative writing workshop in Primrose Hill. We've got a new Australian teacher now who wants us to do some awful Australian thing, *Under the Eucalyptus Tree*, or something like that. Have the essay done by Friday. What's on telly?'

'Have you got the play?'

'That's not a play. It's a – I can't describe it, it's a ghastly sort of rubbish thing.'

'Well whatever it is, can I see it?'

'No. I left it on the bus. Just write anything. He's only a supply teacher, so he won't mind what you say. He probably won't even be there next Friday.'

I stared at the telly with glazed, unseeing eyes. The eyes of a newsreader stared back, blandly unaware that my masterpiece was lost to the world, forever unappreciated.

I am beginning to suspect I am more indebted to God than I had previously imagined.

RANT

LOUIS BARFE *can't bear uncivil travellers*

ONE MORNING recently, I caught a train. And, as usual, I had my bicycle and was cutting it fine. I raced towards the carriage where bikes are carried, but the guard told me that the train was full and I would have to leave it behind. I rushed to lock up, then got on the train, expecting to see the massed Claud Butlers of a cycling club on their way to an Alpine jaunt.

Instead, I saw a father with a child in a pushchair, a morbidly obese man on an electric disability cart and a pile of

suitcases. I went from nought to fuming in three seconds, incensed by the general tendency to regard public transport as private transport.

Parents with buggies who refuse to fold them up are one example, but others abound. I recently sat, on a packed-to-bursting express, near a couple who put their suitcases on the seats next to them while other passengers stood. My remonstrations fell on deaf ears. They felt they had a divine right to hog the seats. It would have taken a saint not to cheer when they were fined for invalid tickets.

I also baulked at the implicit idea that obesity is a proper disability. It isn't. I'm 17 stone, and I know why – pies. So, I cycle, walk and swim. I recently saw a profoundly fat man sitting in the middle of a muddy park in his electric chariot, smoking and waiting for the Fire Brigade to pull him out. Naturally, it wasn't his fault for attempting to drive his 30 stone across a quagmire, nor was he wasting the firemen's valuable time, and, had I asked, I'm confident that he would have declared his size was a 'glandular' issue rather than the result of refusing to walk anywhere. Move along the car, please. If you can.

L ady Williams of Elvel is so deliciously courteous that, meeting this lively and attractive 76-year-old, one might easily think that one was the most fascinating person she had ever encountered. It is the daftest of impressions, given that she worked for the man declared the Greatest Briton ever.

After Churchill became PM again in 1951, Williams was one of three secretaries he took with him to Number 10 (he paid her £405 a year).

'He often had evening engagements but would be back working in the Cabinet Room by 10.30pm, and would go on dictating until 1am or 2am, after which I would type everything up before going home, and then I would be back again at 10am the next day. I spent alternate weekends working at Chartwell, where one of the duties I loved was to choose the Friday and Saturday night films. I would be working 12 days out of 14, and until two am four or five nights a week. But I was young and I never thought it was peculiar.'

In late 1949 Lady W – then Miss Jane Portal – had finished a secretarial course and was living with her mother's brother, the future Chancellor of the Exchequer, Rab Butler, and his wife in their house in Westminster. Rab mentioned that Churchill was looking for a junior secretary. A brief interview with the great man followed and the job was hers. Air Marshal Lord Portal was another uncle – her father's brother – and a great favourite of Churchill's in the war.

Despite these connections, Lady W started, as she says, 'right at the bottom' – in two senses of the word. For the first two months she was filing Churchill's correspondence in the semi-basement of his London home, 28 Hyde Park Gate.

'The windows looked up towards the front door,' she says, 'so I was used to seeing the bottom halves of everyone , and would recognise people from their appearance below the waist. Anthony Eden was one I easily identified from his beautifully tailored trousers.'

On the never-to-be-forgotten day that she took her first dictation from Churchill, it was mid-morning, and he was in his bedroom at Hyde Park Gate, preparing a major speech on world affairs for delivery in the Commons at an hour that was fast approaching.

'All the other secretaries were busy, and I was told I would have to go and take dictation. Being only 20, I was terrified. I went upstairs and there he was, this mythical figure, lying in bed in his dressing gown, a cigar in his mouth, and

Not just anybody

SUE CORBETT *talks to Lady Williams of Elvel, whose job as secretary to Churchill taught her the secrets of an energetic old age – and how to recognise politicians from the waist down... Portrait by* **JANE BOWN**

the bed strewn with papers and pets.'

Churchill loathed any changes to his secretarial line-up. So when this young creature, whom he knew only from the briefest of interviews months before, appeared at his door at such a crucial moment, it was lucky that he said only 'Isn't there anybody else?' and not something even more crushing. Even so, Lady W fled in dismay.

'But the other secretaries sent me back again. When I returned, Churchill was very friendly towards me as if to make up for it, and I like to think that, after that, we never looked back.'

Churchill was in his mid-seventies then, but he organised his energy well. He worked in bed in the mornings, but would get up in good time for lunch, after which he would be driven to the House of Commons. 'One of us secretaries was always with him in the car,' says Lady W. 'Even on the way from Number 10 to the Speaker's Entrance, he would aim to dictate a couple of minutes to ministers.'

Lady W was also in the car that took Churchill, as PM, to the then London Airport, to welcome the young Queen Elizabeth II home from Kenya after the sudden death of King George VI. 'All the way there he was dictating to me the content of his broadcast to the nation later that day, in which he talked about the King's death and Her Majesty's accession, and he was very much moved,' she says. 'When we got to the airport the flight was just coming in and I remember going with Eden's private secretary, Evelyn Shuckburgh, to crouch behind the wheels of an aeroplane parked nearby and see the Queen, this beautiful young girl, come out of the aeroplane.'

She also took dictation from Churchill while he was sitting for the controversial Graham Sutherland portrait. 'I never saw the original because the artist covered it

'I was told I would have to go and take dictation from Churchill. I was absolutely terrified. Churchill said only: "Isn't there anybody else?"'

up at the end of each sitting. But when I saw a colour photograph, I was horrified and told Churchill: "It's not you." It was a painting of an old man, looking depressed, and the man whose dictation I had taken while it was being painted was not like that at all, but was energetic, totally with it and animated.'

Churchill's eventual retirement in 1955 coincided with Lady W's first marriage, and there was a parting of the ways. But the marriage didn't last and Churchill was soon arranging for her to be the go-between between him and the American Broadcasting Company (ABC) to make sure that all the details in *The Valiant Years*, a TV series based on his war memoirs, were correct.

As production secretary, Lady W was based in ABC's Jermyn Street office. Part of her job was to go on *The Valiant Years* shoots and, from her knowledge of Churchill, point out inexactitudes. 'For one close-up of him writing, they were going to show his hands as podgy. I said they should find a double with long, beautiful hands and get the signet ring right.'

She also conducted some of the interviews, quizzing the novelist J B Priestley at his Albany apartment and being taken by him to dinner at The Ivy.

More film work followed, with job offers from ABC and John Schlesinger. Then, in the mid 1960s, the co-producer of *The Valiant Years*, Bob Graff, employed Lady W on his film *Young Cassidy*, about the life of Sean O'Casey.

After several years in films, Lady W embarked on a change of career and trained as a probation officer to join the probation service in 1970 in south London.

'In those days borstal boys had to earn their release by good behaviour. I would visit them first and get to know them, and then, after their release, they had a statutory six months of aftercare during which I would try to find them jobs in shops or places on literacy courses. I also used to help get them into the armed forces, though there were strictures: they knew it would be one fault and they were out.

'I had a case-load of eighty and the hours were terrible, especially the evenings as that's when you see your clients. But when I married my second husband, Charles Williams, in 1975, he said of course I was to go on with it if I wanted.

'I realised, though, that I couldn't combine probation work with newly married life, so in 1976 I became a magistrate. I didn't enjoy that so much because I felt I was sitting there doling out punishment without knowing enough detail. But then I was on the Parole Board for six years and absolutely loved it.'

Now retired, Lady W does voluntary work. 'I'm a trustee of a project that is very, very dear to my heart, called Kids VIP. We work with the prison service and other organisations to sustain and develop relationships between imprisoned parents and their children. And there are now only 20 prisons in the whole country where we don't operate. I also help run charity events for Macmillan Cancer Relief because I had cancer but recovered and feel I owe them a debt.

'Now that I am much the same age as Churchill when I first worked for him, I can see in my grandchildren's lovely faces, and the way they take care of me, that they think I'm old! But I'm lucky because I am incredibly energetic and I have a full life. I suppose I am conscious of pacing myself, much as Churchill did when he dictated from bed in the mornings. But, unlike Churchill, I'm exhausted if I've stayed up till midnight.'

The ghosts of Norfolk

Those footsteps seemed to be following DR THOMAS STUTTAFORD around...

Few interests also provide an income. Forty-five years ago, restoring crumbling Grade I or Grade II houses did. The first of six houses I salvaged was a Victorian Gothic rectory faced in knapped Norfolk flints and with tall barley-stick chimneys. I was still working in London and needed to leave immediately after my outpatients' surgery in order to reach the old rectory while it was light and the builders were still working overtime.

One day I sped down from London and reached the village before dusk, but there was only the site foreman, a former RN petty officer, to greet me. He told me that his jolly band of hard-working bricklayers, plumbers, carpenters and electricians had refused to stay on lest they were caught in the house after dusk.

They had been troubled for a week or two by footsteps all over the house. They thought it was the locals trying to nick their tools, but they could never see them, let alone catch them. Finally the petty officer hatched a plan. They waited downstairs until they heard someone come in at the front door, climb the stairs and wander around the first floor. The builders split into three parties. One party surrounded the front and back of the house while the other two searched the house in best military fashion. It was empty.

The first two or three weeks after we moved in were slightly unnerving. My wife and I slept on the first floor and my brother-in-law, a serious psychiatrist, was staying in the attic. In the middle of his first night there he rushed down to ask what I thought I was doing. Regularly throughout the early hours he had heard me climb the stairs to the attic and walk along the corridor to his room; then the footsteps just disappeared. I assured him that I hadn't been outside my room all night. He left.

My aunt-in-law was the next to stay. She was a delightful but sensitive eccentric. I thought that we must have offended her as she became increasingly tense. She lasted three days, and then just disappeared. She came back again

after a day or two and told me she had resolved that at her age she would have to take what this or the next world had to throw at her. She didn't mind the footsteps too much, decided she could just stand the noise of a chair being scraped across her floor (it was in fact carpeted), but drew the line at the noise of her window opening and shutting.

Oh Auntie, don't be so melodramatic — it's just some old timbers creaking!

A man in dark clothing could be seen flitting around the edges of the room, and there was the sound of a Sanctus bell

About a month later I was working in the library and the rest of the family was in the nursery watching television. I heard the cellar door open and the noise of someone moving around in the boiler room beneath me. Eventually, fearing that one of the children might be playing dangerously close to wires and electrical equipment, I went into the nursery. They were all still there and watching television. 'What were you doing down in the cellar, Doctor?' asked the children's nanny. I assured her that I had not been down there.

And so it went on: footsteps, noises of

furniture being moved, doors opening and shutting and lights being switched on and off. These phenomena were all witnessed by people who knew nothing of them, and volunteered their experiences. Our kindly local parson began to arrange exorcism, but after consideration we decided that we had become so accustomed to the ghostly footsteps that we wouldn't bother.

I never saw anything untoward, but a neighbour told me that one day she had seen an old woman walking over our paddock when the apparently solid stranger suddenly disappeared.

Our successor in the house, a retired regular army officer, was unconcerned other than finding that the footsteps kept him awake. Finally he banged on the ceiling above the bedroom and said, 'I'm a good Catholic and so the afterlife has no fear for me. On the other hand, while still in this world I have to work in the morning. In the name of Christ, go.' Thereafter peace reigned. Even so, his daughter, an apparently equally phlegmatic Wren officer, confided that she would never stay in the house alone. Later owners of the house had terrible problems, but that is another story and it is their story.

My other heavily haunted house was Snore Hall in West Norfolk. It is the fifth oldest brick house in the country and was built in the early 1480s. It is a Catholic house, with a chapel in the attic and priest-holes and connecting tunnels that run from top to bottom as well as across it. In the 16th century the owners became prosperous tobacco importers and enlarged the house. It was at Snore at the end of the Civil War that Charles I met his councillors and took the decision to surrender.

The additions were later burnt down, but we lived in the original 15th-century building. Later Snore Hall was sold to Iain Sproat, the former Conservative minister. While he was living there the *Sunday Telegraph* devoted a whole page, rather to his chagrin, to its hauntings, which included the sound of Protestant

'Do you think you'll ever get married again?'

forces approaching and searching the house for the resident priest.

While we were there we experienced, just as at our old rectory, monotonously regular inexplicable footsteps, but we also had sightings and other sounds. In the dining-room a man in dark clothes could be seen flitting around the edges of the room, and there was the occasional sound of a Sanctus bell, though there was neither clock nor bell in the room. In the main guest bedroom an old woman in white came to look at any child who was staying. We were aware of none of these stories when we moved in, nor was Iain Sproat when he went there, but our experiences were remarkably similar.

A strange twist to the ghostly nanny occurred when a journalist colleague came to stay with her three-year-old son, Nicholas. The journalist, who knew nothing of our ghosts, looked over to her son during the night and was astounded to see an elderly woman in white bending over him. The 'nanny' suddenly disappeared. When my colleague came down to breakfast the next day she asked, 'Do you think that your house could be haunted? I saw an elderly woman in a long white gown bending over Nicholas.' Thereafter we could never meet strangers with small children without my children nudging me and whispering, 'Daddy, ask them to stay – ghost bait.'

My own children were not enthusiastic to volunteer as ghost-hunters. On one occasion when they were rather older, the ghosts had been so active that they decided between them that the best thing to do was to arm themselves and lock themselves into the bathroom.

Snore Hall in our time had spectral smells as well as auditory and visual manifestations. The house frequently reeked of tobacco, but none of us smoked. Whether the 16th-century half-timbered extension was burnt down as the result of smoking is unknown.

'I think we should start bickering, I don't want people to think we're soulmates'

RANT

I'll tell you what I can't stand. Interactive radio and TV. In the 1990s I tuned to Radio 2 to escape from Chris bloody Evans. Now Chris bloody Evans is on Radio 2, and boasting the most 'interactive' show on the radio. We don't just sit and listen to him spouting shit anymore, now we can all join in!

The idea is that we, the listeners, send in our texts and emails to be read out on air. You expect to hear the general public talking out of their behinds on Jeremy Vine's lunchtime phone-in, but now all the DJs are at it. 'Text in and tell me the funniest thing that ever happened to you.' 'Text in and tell us where you are and what you're doing.' No matter how inane or trivial the responses, the chances are

No matter how inane or trivial the responses, the chances are they'll be read out on air

they'll be read out on air. Gary in Essex says he's driving a van on the A34. Well, bully for you, Gary.

I was watching football on Channel 5 the other day and the commentator asked for my comments on the game so far. No! YOU are the commentator. You commentate on the football match. I am the person sitting at home watching the bloody television, thank you very much.

I suppose you can understand it on commercial TV. They're just trying to make a fast buck out of slow viewers with mobile phone addictions. But the benevolent BBC actually thinks it's doing us a favour by opening up the airwaves. Why should broadcasting be the exclusive preserve of talented broadcasters? Now we can all 'have our say'. That's a bit like a bus driver asking if anyone else fancies driving for a while. After all, why should he hog the steering wheel?

As a result Radio 2 is slowly being transformed into a giant third-rate commercial radio phone-in. And Chris from Newcastle has just switched off.
CHRIS DONALD

To London on a very early train, the countryside lush and empty. It was going to be a warm, sunny day. Hardly anyone on the streets, no flags, no bunting, no sign that today would mark the end of six years of living in the dark – bombed-out, blacked-out – at times with no end in sight. Surely Londoners were going to do more than have a lie in?

* * *

Thoroughly depressed, we had breakfast in an empty restaurant that leaned on the Odeon Cinema. We perked up with the sudden appearance of an old man, an old horse and a cart loaded with flags that he proceeded to arrange as carefully as a woman doing the flowers. The whooping GIs whizzed past me in a jeep, then the landgirls. It was going to be all right.

* * *

Misled by images still running through our minds of explosions of joy, exultant European crowds, girls rushing to kiss triumphant soldiers, we were not expecting quiet people to slowly fill the streets, like patients going out for the first time, blinking, surprised and pleased, walking out of a bad dream, checking out reality and memories, gaining confidence; recovering Londoners recovering their city.

Turning the lights back on

JANET TOURNIERE *remembers the mixed emotions of VE Day, which she also captured in her sketchbook 60 years ago*

THOUSANDS SQUEEZING into Whitehall, pushing and squeezing.

I panicked. If I trip, I'll be trampled to death. Churchill. Cheers. I hear words. I'll die if I fall. At 3pm the war is over. We are at peace. Rather tired. Relaxing. The mood lightened. Satisfaction after a good job done.

Boarded up Eros was the centre of the freed world. We forgot all about the phases of the moon

NIGHT WAS THE best part of that day. Electricity, lights, fireworks, flashing Piccadilly ads switched on, floodlights, light – no longer treasonable – streaming from open windows. Bonfires. Boarded up Eros was the centre of the freed world. We forgot all about the phases of the moon.

Left and above: Impressions of VE Day by Janet Tourniere; Below: Outside the National Gallery by D K Leet, Janet's companion on her trip to London

Child of Beacon Hill

DAVID BOSWELL'S *father was a keen follower of Bertrand Russell and sent David to Russell's Beacon Hill school. But it wasn't long before rebellion set in...*

Shortly before my parents' divorce in 1927 I was despatched to boarding school at the age of four-and-a-half. As my father was a keen disciple of Bertrand Russell, I was sent to his newly formed Beacon Hill School in deepest Sussex. Russell hoped that Beacon Hill would provide 'a really modern education which, instead of training young children to maintain every prejudice of traditional society, or teaching them new dogmas, should try to help them to think and work for themselves.'

Among my fellow pupils were Russell's two children, John and Kate. Dora Russell – not yet Lady Russell – was in charge. She was a very short woman with, as I was later to discover, a distinctive odour in bed.

My mother came to say goodbye while father stood in the background. It was afternoon siesta on one of the lawns. We lay on camp beds and she did not kiss me, but bent over me, patted me and waved as she went. I did not understand what was happening or what it meant. Other children watched us, and I did not cry.

Telegraph House was a dour stone building with a central tower overlooking the surrounding wilderness. Built atop a hill on the South Downs, it lay between the villages of East Harting and Elsted and was approached by a mile-long private drive from the southern edge of the estate. There were several lawns surrounding the buildings, but beyond them were bracken, scrub and gorse bushes. There were some areas of woodland but few pathways. It was as I imagined Dartmoor prison might be – I did escape once with a friend, but we were recaptured.

The rooms had very high ceilings and there was an annexe to the north of the main building which was the communal eating room. Bertrand Russell had his office at the top of the tower – an ideal place in which to write mathematical and philosophical treatises. It was approached via a step-ladder through a hole in the ceiling – like a loft.

Bertrand Russell had his office at the top of the tower which was approached via a step-ladder through a hole in the ceiling

The main schoolmistress was a marvellous lady, Beatrix Tudor-Hart, who later ran the well-known Fortis Green Nursery School in north London. She became a close friend of our family for many years until the war led to a parting of the ways.

I think my father was in love with her. My first memory of her was when she diagnosed that I had flat feet and I was made to walk barefoot round the front lawn on the outer edges of my soles several times a day in summer. I am not sure it did any good and it probably exacerbated my bandy legs. It did make me feel as though I was different from the other schoolchildren, of whom there were a dozen, maybe fifteen.

As well as being boarding, Beacon Hill was small and co-educational – it may have been one of the first in England at that time. We were allowed a mid-morning break in which we could go where we liked. On one such excursion about four of us crept into a gorse bush area near the house. We all undressed and became fully acquainted with the physical differences between girls and boys – at our lower extremities, that is.

Another landmark was an afternoon expedition on horseback. Half a dozen of us were riding in procession through the bracken when my horse moved rapidly ahead of the one in front – which objected to this sudden spurt and lunged forward to bite me gently on the right bum. I fell screaming to the ground. The penetration was negligible, but I have always boasted that I have permanent horse-bite marks to show for my pains.

Every Sunday evening Bertrand Russell invited us all up the step-ladder into his study at the top of the tower. He read us stories and gave us hot cocoa and ginger biscuits. It was a treat we loved and looked forward to, but I cannot recall a single story.

My dormitory on the first floor was shared with four other children of a similar age. At about five o'clock one summer morning we all woke early with the sun streaming in, but did not realise the time. A unanimous decision was taken to play 'elephants' – which consisted of jumping from bed to floor, on to the next bed, then to the floor, and so on, in quick succession all round the room. We had not been playing very long when the dormitory door swung open and Dora Russell appeared, white-faced, in her nightgown. She grabbed the nearest elephant – me – marched me downstairs to her bedroom, lifted me over a pile of broken glass and metal and threw me onto her bed.

Her bedroom was directly below our dormitory and our elephants jumping game had caused a giant chandelier to leave its moorings on the ceiling below. It had come crashing down within inches of her head. Another foot or so and she would not have survived. She climbed into bed with her back to me and attempted or pretended to go to sleep. I was petrified, but my enduring memory of those two hours is her body odour. I can still smell her to this day. At least I can claim to have slept with Lady Russell.

I was thought to be the ringleader, and the following day I was removed from the dormitory and despatched to sleep in the small gatehouse at the end of the mile-long entrance drive. It was a sort of isolation ward, run by a strict nanny who lived there. I think she was the wife or mistress of Hans, Russell's German chauffeur.

My enduring memory of those two hours is Bertrand Russell's wife Dora's body odour. I can still smell her to this day

Opposite, top: Russell in the grounds of Beacon Hill school with pupils
Bottom: Telegraph House
Above: Russell & Dora

I found this quite exciting because every morning at eight o'clock Hans had to drive me to the mansion in the big posh car for breakfast and take me back again in the early evening after school supper. After some weeks he took pity on me and let me sit beside him and hold the steering wheel as we drove along. It was heaven. One morning he allowed me to hold the wheel as we passed the main lawn in front of the house. I gave it a sudden heave and before he could regain control we were cruising over the rain-sodden lawn, the heavy car making deep ruts in a beautiful sward for what must have been the length of a cricket pitch. It was a sorry sight. I was sentenced to a prolonged stay in the lodge house and banned from driving.

The following summer, an American girl and I made an expedition into nearby bracken and gorse bushes during a free break period. One of us had acquired a box of matches and we set fire to the bracken and ran back to the school.

Not many minutes later there was a hubbub. Fire brigades from five counties were needed to stifle the blaze and at one time the whole building was under threat.

The following morning I was having my breakfast in the dining room. The only telephone was quite near my table, and I could hear the stentorian voice of Bertrand Russell telling my father to come at once and fetch his 'dreadful child'. I had been expelled.

Bertrand Russell later claimed that I started the fire because I was jealous of a girl who had a rabbit. I deny this. We did start the fire not far from the rabbit hutches, but I believe it was my simple cry for help: 'Get me out of here. I want my mother and my brother.'

I don't know whether the estate was insured against the folly of its young pupils. Fifty years later I wrote to Bertrand Russell at his home in Wales apologising for my bad conduct and explaining that, despite my problems, I had achieved my ambition of 'contributing in life'. His reply surprised me: it was an apology for the shortcomings of his school.

'I have your husband here. He says he's glad he's dead'

Power behind the crone

FLORA HINTON *remembers a time when the real movers and shakers in business were not the high-powered executives, but the old biddies with the tea trollies...*

Where are the crones? There was at least one in every office before the new technology and obsession with youth took hold. In the late sixties and early seventies I was assistant story editor in a film company in Soho, and by far the most powerful people in the building, populated though it was by famous, rich old has-beens and streetwise young hustlers (now venerated auteurs), were the three middle-aged biddies who operated the tea-urn and the mailroom. (And Mr Stoddart, more of whom later.) Despite the fact that secretaries wore hot-pants, where in more conventional organisations women were forbidden even to wear trousers, and young men wore floppy hair, jeans and an air of jaded knowingness, Ivy, Mary, and Mrs Holder were the people to know. In fact, if you didn't know them, your time there was never going to amount to anything very much.

Mrs Holder, who ruled the mailroom, was never known by her first name, unlike her sister, Ivy (half of the

tea-urn team), or her husband, Alf, who was senior messenger and occasional chauffeur to the mighty. Between them, the family had most angles covered. Mrs Holder had deep-dyed black hair, impermeable make-up and pretentions to gentility, and pronounced her husband's name as 'Elf', which at first I took to be his nickname – he was tiny and shy, whereas Mrs Holder

The Christmas club was a protection racket in all but name, and you opted out at your peril

was neither. She sat like a spider in her airless room, spinning tales outwards and reeling in tasty morsels captured by her spies, and left her centre of operations only once a week, on payday, when she processed round the building collecting premiums for her notorious Christmas Club. £1 a week (plus an extra 6d for her trouble) meant that when divvying-up time came round you had £52 to spend on presents, a moderately princely sum in those days, and Mrs Holder was entitled to everyone's accumulated sixpences plus the interest on the principal. The more that went in, the greater the profit for Mrs Holder, so refusal to enlist in the Club was a personal insult to her. It was a protection racket in all but name, and you opted out at your peril. Takings were banked weekly, and the force of her insistence on showing bank statements to prove that everything was

above-board was such that it gave rise to an unvoiced suspicion that she was up to no good. Unfounded, of course, I must make that clear. Very clear. Even so, more than 30 years on, I am writing under a *nom de plume*.

Ivy and Mary were, by the nature of their duties, more peripatetic. The trolley came round daily at 11am and 3.15pm, and you welcomed their stewed tea and flaccid biscuits with a show of real enthusiasm if you had any sense. They went everywhere and saw everything, soaking up, embellishing and redistributing stories of feuds, liaisons, takeovers, makeovers, secrets and lies. Their coarse jokes and irreverent banter made them fearfully popular, and you trembled as they passed, well aware that your craven camaraderie was nothing but grist to their mill once they got back to base.

I include Mr Stoddart the stationery-cupboard manager because he was, effectively, an honorary crone. He wore a starched white coat like a first-year medical student and lived with his unmarried daughter in Billericay. His sphere of influence, although narrow, was intensely focused, as he was able on petty grounds to refuse supplies of almost anything he pleased. 'Correction fluid?' he would sneer. 'Planning to make a few mistakes, are we?' His bitterness originated, apparently, in blighted attempts to win prizes for his pelargoniums at the Essex County Show, but flannelling offers of sympathy were firmly rebuffed. (He was sometimes referred to as 'the ink monitor', a reference meaningful only to a genuine oldie.)

I miss them. What has taken their place? More importantly, where are those jobs? Just when I am ripe for turning into Mrs Holder myself, the ideal employment for my declining years has vanished beyond my grasp.

ILLUSTRATIONS BY GRIZELDA GRIZLINGHAM

No siesta, señora

NICHOLAS GORDON LENNOX, *former British ambassador to Spain, remembers the Thatchers' visit to Madrid in the eighties – and the former prime minister's scorn...*

We had two visits from Mrs Thatcher while I was the British ambassador in Madrid. The first was the only time a British prime minister had ever visited Spain officially. She arrived with her husband, Denis, and her close team of familiars – Charles Powell and Bernard Ingham. The idea was to discuss matters of common concern, Gibraltar and the European Community being, of course, high on the list of contentious issues.

She arrived late one evening having flown from Bruges, where the previous day she had made the now celebrated speech defining Britain's attitude at the time (or hers at any rate) to the European Community. We had supper, and afterwards I briefed her on the next day's programme. To my consternation she yawned and her eyes began to close.

She was obviously very tired. I raised my eyebrows at Charles Powell, her private secretary, and he whispered, 'Don't worry, she will be perfectly okay in the morning.' She was. It is true that she only needed a few hours' sleep at night.

The next day I took her on the sort of visit which prime ministers do on these occasions. She went to see the King and had a long session with Prime Minister Felipe González, with whom she had a vigorous argument about Gibraltar, not always getting her facts right. My Spanish opposite number in London and I sat in on the meeting as uneasy spectators, both wishing that the two principals could find more on which to agree.

Then there was a luncheon hosted by the Spanish Prime Minister. I suppose about thirty of us were seated on separate round tables. Mrs Thatcher sat next to the Spanish Prime Minister on one side, but they had no common language. I sat a little further down, next to the Prime Minister's wife, a pretty lady who was a secondary school teacher. One of the ambassador's roles on these occasions is to keep the conversational ball rolling, and Señora de González talked to me about her teaching, saying that she was having a rest for one year to give greater support to her husband. I said: 'Mrs González is a secondary school teacher but is having a rest for one year to give her time to help with her husband's duties.' Mrs Thatcher reacted

To my consternation Mrs Thatcher yawned and her eyes began to close. 'Don't worry, she'll be perfectly okay in the morning'

strongly to this, her eyes blazing. 'Rest!' she said. 'Rest! You tell Mrs González from me that I have been an MP now for over 25 years and I don't need a rest!' As so often, I found myself having to turn the words around in Spanish so they sounded at least polite. In the end, Mrs Thatcher and Mr González both made friendly and agreeable speeches and the luncheon broke up.

On our way to see the Spanish Prime Minister before lunch, I said to Mrs Thatcher, 'The Prime Minister is, as you know, also head of the Spanish Socialist Party, but he is very much not the sort of Socialist you and I know, more of a Social Democrat.' Mrs Thatcher said, 'Don't tell me that,' adding, 'I know all these people, they are all the same.'

Then I took her to the Spanish '*Cortes*', or Parliament, where there was a meeting with leaders of the political parties. It threw up few points of interest until she came to Nicolas Sartorius, a member of an old and distinguished Spanish family. Nicolas made some remarks which revealed his sympathies; although relatively young, and an aristocrat, he had for some time been head of the Spanish Communist Party. 'I have heard all this from the Soviet leadership,' said Mrs Thatcher, with a touch of acidity. It was clear that the other party leaders appreciated her point of view as she got a standing ovation when she left, which cheered her up a lot. She was very happy to have been so well received and applauded.

On the way back to her car, discreetly parked not too far away, she met a 'spontaneously' assembled group of Spanish boys and girls from the excellent British Council School and chatted to them briefly. She also received greetings from elderly spectators or passers-by, the sort who sat on park benches with cigarettes dangling from their lower lip, either reading tabloid newspapers or just sitting. I don't think she understood what they were saying. Their line was mostly that Spain needed a strong leader, like her, like Franco. She liked that too.

The last meeting I organised for her was about a dozen people, mostly Spanish businessmen with views on economic and financial matters or captains of Spanish industry. I agreed with Charles Powell that we would have general conversation before lunch, until the start of the first course when I would ask one of the Spanish guests to embark on a theme in which Mrs Thatcher would like to join, and which with luck would provoke a discussion.

I therefore got hold of Miguel Boyer, the ex-Minister for Economics, and he readily agreed to kick off a discussion of this kind at the appropriate time. Unfortunately, he chose as his theme

> **When, finally, Boyer had finished speaking, there was a silence and Mrs Thatcher said, 'So what?'. It was an awkward and chilling moment...**

Third World debt, with particular reference to South America, a subject for which Mrs Thatcher had contempt and certainly no interest whatsoever. When, finally, Boyer had finished speaking, there was a silence and Mrs Thatcher said, 'So what?'. It was an awkward and chilling moment, and another challenge for the ambassador's conversational persiflage, but happily one of my other guests then seized the initiative and started off on another topic in which Mrs Thatcher did display an interest.

For some reason Mrs Thatcher did not seem to like being out of doors.

My wife Mary tried to persuade her that it would be nice to have dinner in the garden or, later, to be photographed there with the embassy domestic staff. She seemed to resist this and we wondered why. She was evidently one of those people who preferred to operate in a confined space.

Denis Thatcher, a very nice man, was magnificent in his support of her. Mary took him on and did some sightseeing with him, fuelling him from time to time with gin and tonics ('No ice in it, please, dear').

He was polite and accommodating at all times, but I do not think he much appreciated Picasso's Guernica, which had become a symbol for Republicans in the Civil War, and which we took him to see as one of the sights of Madrid. He muttered that this was not really his style, and I am sure he meant what he said.

Although always a courteous guest, Mrs Thatcher was not big on small talk, and in two days she never asked Mary a single question about Spain and her life in it. She was focused, and the focus was not on politics in Spain, but mostly in England.

When she finally left, by air, she thanked me and said, 'Your Mr González is a very impressive person.' It was nice to hear that, but the 'your' made it sound a little as if I was in Spanish pay, not hers. She wrote me a very polite and complimentary letter afterwards.

LOOKS LIKE THUNDER

SHE ALWAYS DOES

RANT

SOME OF MY best friends are members of book clubs. (Though once I know they are, I tend to look at them as warily as when I suddenly learn that friends are, actually, Catholics. The information puts a whole different slant on them, I find.)

But for me the whole idea of a book club is hell. Who in their right mind wants to sit in a room full of middle-aged women drinking cups of tea, discussing books? Books (I always thought) are for reading, not for discussing. Perhaps sitting in a room discussing books reminds them of the days when they were young, discussing Bertrand Russell in cramped digs at university? But surely, now we're old, we don't want to be reminded of being young, or of days at university. A mature woman of my age (62) should want to spend her time doing old things, not young things – like gardening, taking drugs for the first time (much more sensible when you're older) or simply staring out of the window, something I haven't had time to do in the whole of my conscious life.

And then, my dear, it's not only the people, but the books! Who honestly wants to read *Captain Corelli's Mandolin? Jane Eyre? The God of Small Things? The Bookseller of Kabul?* A frightful mixture of trendy contemporary novels and whacked-out old classics. Surely these people have more interesting things to do with their final hours than wasting four of them wading through a badly-written book that they don't enjoy – with the one aim of criticising it later?

I suspect that most people who join book clubs do it because they feel that they have to prod their brains with a pointed stick every week to keep it active. But a) there are other ways of keeping it alive, like reading more books rather than discussing them, and b) if you have an active brain, prodding it with a stick will just weary it, not stimulate it.

Book clubs are also so determinedly uncreative. Knitting would be far, far more interesting – don't sneer. Once you get to four needles, knitting knocks Sudoku into a cocked hat when it comes to brain stimulation. And, most important, at least you have something interesting and useful to show for it in the end.

VIRGINIA IRONSIDE

A Knight to remember

LUCY LETHBRIDGE'S *first experience of a naked man was in the unlikely setting of a talk by Shakespearean scholar Sir George Wilson Knight...*

Apart from a tantalising glimpse of a streaker in the woods, the first time I saw a naked man he was standing on a stage in front of an amazed audience of teenage schoolchildren. It was the early 1980s, I was a convent schoolgirl, and the naked figure was Sir George Wilson Knight, author of *The Wheel of Fire*, and many other seminal works of Shakespearean criticism. He was in his mid-eighties.

My boarding school was stuck away down a very long drive in rural Surrey and there wasn't much to do in the evenings except crowd round one small television with 150 other girls. So when six of us were offered the chance by our inspiring English teacher, Miss Jenkins, to go and see Sir George give a talk on Shakespeare, it offered a tempting diversion. Most exciting of all was the fact that the event was to take place in a boys' school – Dulwich College.

We travelled by minibus, all six of us glistening with freshly applied passion-fruit lip potion, Miss Jenkins at the wheel. On arrival, we took our places in the school hall among a sea of adolescent boys to whom we feigned indifference.

This talk was obviously a grand occasion, and stops had been pulled out: in honour of Old Alleynian Sir George, there was a mountainous flower arrangement at the front of the stage; the headmaster was looking nervous.

When everyone was seated in respectful hush, a frail, snowy-haired figure in a grey suit appeared on the stage, leaning on a stick, and the Head leapt to his feet and made a speech of welcome, with a great deal of jocular murmurs: 'So proud, so honoured'; 'All the way from Canada' (the great man had taught at the University of Toronto

for many years). The lights dimmed, the Head took his seat and the frail figure began to speak.

Sir George seemed distracted from the very beginning. It was difficult to make out what he was saying as his voice was light and quavery, and a flustered master in the wings hastily adjusted the microphone which then emitted ear-splitting howls. Sir George looked rather bored, muttered a few general words about wheels of fire and flies to wanton boys, then leaned on his stick and, looking straight at the audience, told us that he

Sir George returned to the stage stark naked except for a tiny leather loincloth and a moth-eaten woman's wig

had always wanted to be an actor and now, in his last years, no longer had any desire to talk about Shakespeare but instead wished to act out his favourite tragic roles. With that he walked off the stage.

The headmaster craned his neck into the wings anxiously, the microphone squawked and the audience shuffled their feet. When Sir George returned he was stark naked except for a tiny leather loincloth and a moth-eaten woman's wig. We were stunned into amazed silence, but Wilson Knight appeared to have forgotten our existence: his voice was now an actorly boom, and without bothering with preambles, he launched straight into mad King Lear, hurling his spindly body about and berating nature, gods and man with his walking stick. He went through Hamlet, Othello, Coriolanus and Julius Caesar, clenching his fists, rolling his eyes, beating his breast and obviously enjoying himself enormously. An hour went by. The headmaster looked stricken, the audience was

glued to their seats. Looking back it seems curious that nobody sniggered, but perhaps it was because even we callous adolescents were struck by the poignancy, the tragic pathos, of this aged titan and his hour upon the stage.

Wilson Knight had exhausted all the major roles by the time he reached Timon of Athens, but he went out with a spectacular finale. 'Lower the lights,' he boomed, pointing his walking stick into the wings; the flustered master trained a single spotlight into the darkness. Wilson Knight gazed out at us from beneath his acrylic beehive hairdo: 'This is the moment,' he cried, 'when Timon of Athens abandons civilisation and flees to the woods'; and with that, and a theatrical flourish, the old man pulled at the leather ties of his loincloth; it dropped to the floor and he stood before us – naked completely.

I can't remember exactly what happened next, except that the headmaster clambered onto the stage and, bright red, shook Sir George's hand vigorously, 'Thank you, thank you... I'm sure everyone will agree... absolutely fascinating...' while gesturing to the audience to start applauding immediately – which we did. Unabashed, Wilson Knight took a deep bow, then came forward to accept a bouquet of flowers from the dazed head boy. Smiling happily, waving graciously, he walked off the stage with all the dignity of Irving or Olivier.

In the minibus on the way back to school, we were almost completely silent. There seemed nothing to say, but an awful lot to think about. Navigating the rainy night-time road back to Surrey, Miss Jenkins gripped the steering wheel, looked straight ahead, and said only that she was 'Very, very sorry' that we girls should have had to be witnesses to such a thing. She hoped our parents wouldn't mind.

Years later someone told me that in the last years of his life Wilson Knight quite often took his clothes off: it was a party piece of his. And as to whether I was forever scarred by the experience... Well, only time will tell.

Taking a later train

JANE GARDAM *remembers her first trip to Florence nearly sixty years ago: a magical place, a lifetime away from England and Bovril sandwiches. Illustrations by* **JOHN WARD**

Rabbiting on last January about youthful holidays and the awfulness of air travel today, four of us decided to be 21 again and take a slow train to Florence in the spring. Not on Eurostar. Certainly not on the Orient Express. Just on any old train to Florence that still wanders out of France and into Switzerland and south to blissful Italy. I'd done this in 1949, sitting up all night on a slatted seat with twenty-five pounds in travellers' cheques in a money-belt, and a huge wad of lire worth all of ten pounds.

This time (57 years on) we would book couchettes. First-class couchettes. We have grown old. And we would take substantial luggage, full of nice clothes to wear in good restaurants. The trailing, glorious suede coat of one of us needed a suitcase to itself. So did my Folio Society edition of Arnold Bennett.

The train was to leave from somewhere called Paris-Bercy and the return fare was 400 euros (in 1949 it had been £22). More than any jet, but what the hell? A travel writer friend told us that the train would be wonderful. Linen sheets. Couchettes made up while we dined in the restaurant car. The following morning a steward would wake us with a cup of tea.

Early in May we set off. Our friends had scarcely been to Italy before. My husband's memory of it had faded except for a time at the end of the war when he rode a white stallion and attended an opera in Trieste. These memories seemed unlikely for a Naval Officer. I decided to regale them with my own 1949 journey:

It was June and I was twenty. I had never left England's shores. Only two days before, a college friend and I were writing the last papers of our Finals. The day after that we had been shredded twice over by our basilisk-eyed tutor, and in the afternoon by our Principal, Miss Geraldine Jebb, for arranging to leave before the end of term and telling nobody. ('Have you no loyalty to the college?') We had both wept.

And so, the next day, had my noble mother on Victoria Station, waving us off. She had undertaken to get all my college possessions back to Yorkshire. She too had never been 'abroad'. She had scarcely been to London. She felt I was too young to travel without a duenna. There is a snapshot somewhere of Mary Monk-Jones and I beside the train, very lanky, thin and plain, with long bag-shaped haversacks hanging limply down our backs.

We changed at Dover for the rolling main and sailed to Calais, and here was France for the first time. England behind us was still a shambles from the war and Calais in front of us looked a total ruin. Yet as we steamed across the pallid Pas-de-Calais the fields were looking trim and gents in blue blouses were examining vegetables planted in very straight rows.

Paris next. The Gare du Nord, cloudy with steam and raucous with uninterpretable porters demanding uninterpretable tips. (We gave them nothing because we only had lire.) It sent pleasures down the spine.

The modest luggage was packed away, our seats were found, and then at least twelve French people exploded into the compartment, shook hands with us and sat down. They talked so intimately together that I asked if they were all of the same family, and they looked non-plussed and said no. Then we

'It's bad news I'm afraid, Mr Hall. I've been having an affair with your wife'

Has someone stolen your car?

asked if they were going as far as Milan too, and they looked even more non-plussed, shook hands with us again and fell out of the train at a suburban stop a few minutes later.

We ate our picnic next. It had been bought in Baker Street the day before, after the final interview with Miss Jebb. It was probably Bovril sandwiches. We fell asleep on the slats and woke hours later to find a German student in steel spectacles glaring at us from another slatted seat. The war had been over four years but we were still uncomfortable with Germans. This one informed us that he too was going to Florence and even to the same pensione. Nobody was pleased. He told us to call him 'Herr' and we did until a couple of weeks later someone said 'Why ever do you call that dead-beat "Sir?"'

A shining dawn, and shining young and clear-eyed Swiss on wooden station platforms. A girl with a fat gold plait down her back and a bright blue skirt. All their faces shone with vitamins and the cream, butter, chocolate we hadn't seen since we were eleven years old. Mary and I walked along the train to an almost empty dining car (cloth table napkins!) and I drank real coffee for the first time and ate flakes of manna straight from heaven, called croissants. With butter! Then I must have gone to sleep again and woke at last to see a landscape of blobby watchful trees standing on a grey-green marsh. Wherever was it? It was wondrously beautiful, and 57 years on I see it still. Was it the industrial valley of the dreary Po?

Phrasebooks open, we changed at Milan, achieved the final train, managed to lose Herr and alighted at Firenze station like thistledown on a pearly, early morning. A line of black horse-drawn carriages stood waiting. The horses wore red and yellow plumes and the drivers black hats and there was a tall whip in its holder. We were helped in and clattered through the empty streets and came to a big brown piazza surrounded by stone steps leading up to colonnades. Along one side of the delicate arches were blue and white medallions: the della

I drank real coffee for the first time and ate flakes of manna straight from heaven, called croissants. With butter!

Robbia Innocenti of the 15th-century Foundling Hospital. In the centre of the square, the bronze equestrian statue of Duke Ferdinand flourishing his sword and staring up at the invisible girl in a window: somebody else's bride. The Browning poem: *The Statue and the Bust.* ('Did you do the Browning question?' asked Mary and I couldn't think what she meant.) Opposite the babies was the colonnade of our

Snapshots of Jane Gardam's Italian adventure

pensione, an archway and a stone stair turning out of sight. We jangled a chain and the door was opened by a girl who seemed to be in an ecstasy at seeing us. She showed us to a vast bedroom with a Brunelleschi coffered ceiling. Two little beds stood miles apart. There were two ewers and basins for washing, two thin towels and an acreage of wood floor. We flung open shutters and saluted the great duke. A single donkey cart crossed the empty square.

The Pensione had been in the same family for years. (It still is.) Since before

E M Forster came looking for a room with a view. Mary and I must have passed some sort of test that summer because a week later we were summoned to meet the founding Signora. She sat in a dark, interior room, nodding her head at us. Above her were two huge etchings

in gold frames: a girl knitting while she minded sheep on a stony hillside and a group of farmers having some sort of auction of cows in a lane. The Signora waved her hand at us. There was an antimacassarish smell.

Two lounging Romeos chased us home to the foot of the stairs and we fell through the door gasping

Each evening we all ate together at a long table with wine jugs set out along it.

I had never tasted wine. The food was meat, and not the whale meat which was the college staple. The pudding was fresh apricots handed round in a bowl and I took two before I realised that even here there was only one each. The shame still lingers.

In the warm evenings we wandered the quiet streets, passed our fingers over crumbling Renaissance frescoes on street corners. Little shops sold something called salami which I'd not heard of and you could buy it by the yard. There were currants and raisins for sale, as many as you could afford. There was a hat shop and one hat in the window with poppies and corn around the brim. I yearned: but it was two pounds. 'You can't mean it?' said Mary Monk-Jones who was not frivolous. 'I do.' 'But it's a fertility symbol. An invitation.' 'I know.'

In the daytime we paced with our guide books and often with two other students from Oxford, stately girls who had just finished their own Finals but who would never have forgotten to tell their college they were leaving before

the end of term. One looked happy, the other sad. On the last day the sad one told me that the other one was about to join an enclosed order of nuns. 'Her mother's dreadfully upset. She wants grandchildren. She makes marmalade.' Odd phrases you remember.

Mary and I went to Fiesole, got drunk on new wine, missed the last bus and walked all the miles home singing and sometimes falling over. The pensione was anxious. 'Herr' glared from a corner. The emergent nun looked unperturbed.

Another night we went round the Piazza della Signoria and two lounging Romeos chased us home to the foot of the stairs and we fell through the door gasping and snivelling. Years later, but not many, Mary said 'Weren't we pathetic!'

The summer drowsed on. On my 21st birthday we were in the first of the four trains home. At midnight on the slats we opened a bottle of Chianti encased in straw and drank to the future.

But I didn't want the future. I wanted now, and Italy. The hat with the poppies and the bearded barley. Works of art nonchalant on street corners. The rose-red Duomo. Michelangelo's 'David' gigantic in its glass-domed shrine.

I wanted a man. An Italian. Preferably a painter who would buy me hats.

We trundled to London from Dover through Kent, deliriously green. To marmalade and church on Sundays. To an achingly empty future and no-one to chase me through twilit streets.

Voice from the Grave

'The ordinary method of replenishing the Party Funds is by the sale of peerages, baronetcies, knighthoods and other honours in return for subscriptions. The traffic is notorious. Everyone acquainted in the smallest degree with the inside of politics knows that there is a market for peerages in Downing Street, as he knows that there is a market for cabbages in Covent Garden; he could put his finger upon the very names of the men who have bought their "honours".'

From The Party System, *by Hilaire Belloc and Cecil Chesterton, 1911. Spotted by The Ed.*

£10 PAID FOR CONTRIBUTIONS

'The Superintendent has lost one of his contact lenses'

Roving reporter

Are hoodies evil or are we just panicking? asks **JOHN SWEENEY**

My son was stopped by the police the other day, twice, at the same place. He was not drunk and disorderly (the Prime Minister's son); he was not carrying illegal drugs (the Foreign Secretary's son); he was not wearing Nazi uniform (the heir to the throne's son); and he was not profiting from Saddam's illegal oil sales (the UN Secretary-General's son).

He was walking to Wimbledon Park. His crime, or potential one, is that he is sixteen, has a ridiculous head of frizzy, curly hair and looks like he might be up to no good.

That's it. He is not a cherub. Nor are many of his friends seraphim. He grunts. His spelling is atrocious, he spends too much time thinking about girls and beer and is exactly no different from his father or grandfather at that age.

But we are in the grip of a moral panic about teenagers, hoodies, and their lack of respect at the moment, and so he and his friends have become a target.

They were watched in the park by a couple of 'undercover' police officers – nicknamed 'undies' – and after a while the police came over and checked everyone out. Someone had a tin of beer and they poured it down the drain. When he came home, he told his mum, and my ex, who would not be afraid if a Bengal tiger popped in for tea, went to the park to remonstrate with the cops. The police were pleasant and affable but said they had received complaints from the Residents' Association.

I hold no brief for Residents' Associations. Nor does she. She pointed out that she was a resident too, and that the park on a warm summer's day was a good place for the kids to hang out. Better out in the fresh air than hanging around her place. (Or mine, for that matter.)

The police have carried on doing their thing. But I am enough of a red-blooded Englishman to believe that things have come to a sorry state if a bunch of teenagers can't hang around in a park, 'kotching' and grunting at each other, with the odd illicit tin of beer between them, without being spied on by undercover police officers or being questioned by the uniformed branch.

Is there no real crime out there? I am so ancient these days, but the only times I get into trouble with the law is when I drive past speed cameras too fast or I stray out of my lawful tube pass zone and have to pay a £10 excess fine. But from what I read in the papers, horrible nasty people still exist and do disgusting things to other people. Aren't they the people the cops should be spying on?

And as for the hoody thing... Hoodies are clever bits of kit that keep the rain off your head. If you are very sad, you can put your hood up the whole time and look sinister. (Kind of.) But they are not inherently evil.

Bluewater Shopping Centre speaks to the real problem: a hypocrisy that blathers on about values but cannot stop itself from cashing in

I have never had any intention of going to the Bluewater Shopping Centre, and their ban on hoodies has reinforced that. One should note that in banning hoodies – but continuing to sell them – Bluewater speaks to the real problem: a disgusting and morally obnoxious hypocrisy that blathers on about values but cannot stop itself from cashing in. They should name it the Hypocritical Greedy Gits Shopping Centre, so that we all know they don't put their cash where their proclaimed values are.

Furthermore, I had the great displeasure to listen to *Any Questions* on the steam wireless, presented by one of the Dimblebys – the little, ex-Trotskyist one, with the speech impediment – and heard a parade of politicians jump on to the hoody moral panic bandwagon. They were pathetic, mean-spirited and profoundly un-English.

Hoodies are not inherently wicked. Moral panics are. Any panic is wrong, because calm judgment is lost and emotional over-reactions take their place. The moral panics about child abuse have caused untold agony to innocent people – and got in the way of tracking down and stopping the real child abusers.

The moral panic about Islamic fundamentalism has meant that we have ripped up and thrown away our age-old liberties, that a man has a right to be charged and tried before he loses his liberty. What was good enough for Alfred the Great's time is good enough for us, and I hope I will live to see the day when Her Majesty's Government no longer stands shoulder to shoulder with the government of, say, Burma on detention without trial.

Corporal Jones in *Dad's Army* got it right. His trademark 'Don't panic,' is the soul of wisdom.

'Please welcome our guest speaker, Sir Reginald fforbes-Pemberton, who, after a distinguished career as a Conservative MP, now leans to the left'

K.J.Lamb

COURTESY GETTY IMAGES

Me and my Spike

What's it like working for a man who asks you to shoot him? **ALICE PITMAN** *talks to* **NORMA FARNES**, *who was Spike Milligan's manager and confidante for 36 years*

'Personal Assistant to show business personality,' read the advertisement which caught Norma Farnes's eye back in 1966. Norma, who was sharing a flat in Kensington with three other girls, decided to apply. When she was told the personality was Spike Milligan, Norma got cold feet. She remembered the stories about Spike from her time at Tyne-Tees Television where she started her working life in 1959. The agency assured her that he was really a very nice man. 'Well maybe he is,' said Norma, 'but I don't want to work for him.'

She arrived for her interview on a bitterly cold day. Spike was sitting behind the desk in his tiny office, wearing a woolly hat and a polo-neck sweater.

The French windows were wide open, and there was no central heating. 'The first thing I said was "It's freezing in here." And he said, "Yes, I know. I don't

Spike and Norma attending Johnny Speight's funeral in 1998 (courtesy Empics)

like Americans."' Norma was perplexed. Then the penny dropped.

'I thought, shall I tell him it was the Italians who invented central heating? No, best not to!'

On the filing cabinet, Norma noticed three cartons of Swoop bird seed. Then half a dozen pigeons swooped down on the window ledge.

'Good morning, lads!' said Spike. He began to introduce them to Norma: 'This here's Hoppity, he's only got one leg...'

'I thought, well he's a bit odd... but he can't be all that bad if he feeds the birds.'

Then Spike said, 'You're awfully thin, aren't you? You've got legs just like Olive Oyl. I wonder who'd want to make love to an elastic band...'

Norma fired back, 'Another elastic band.' 'You'll do for me,' said Spike.

Norma was plunged into the anarchic world of Number 9 Orme Court, where Spike and other great post-war comedy writers like Eric Sykes (who is still there), Johnny Speight, Galton and Simpson had formed a writer's cooperative. She planned on sticking with the job for three months, but stayed with Spike

---

until his death 36 years later. Over this time she became his agent, manager, confidante and loyal friend.

Now aged 71, Norma Farnes is a warm, elegantly attired lady with a quick Yorkshire wit, and a breezy, infectious laugh. Her large ground floor office in Bayswater, where she has been based for forty years, is a fitting testament to the life of one of our funniest, most creative entertainers. Photos and mementos of Spike and his friends pepper the walls (Spike with Eric Sykes, Prince Charles, Peter Sellers...) The room is a museum to his memory, his larger-than-life personality permeating the place to such a degree that it is hard not to sense the emptiness left in his void.

Norma sits behind her desk with its antique telephone ('gift from Spike') and affectionately reminisces about her late employer, a man who was by turns notoriously difficult, delightful, a tyrant, compassionate, and capable of great acts of kindness. The manic depression that famously defined Spike Milligan's personality manifested itself early on in their working relationship. Norma quickly learnt that the best way of coping with 'Spike's rantings' was to ignore them.

'One night,' she recounts, 'Spike was screaming about something or other, and I thought, I can't be doing with this, I'm going home. The next morning Ray Galton said to me, "I think you'll stay here... You've got the Scarlett O'Hara attitude: I'll deal with it tomorrow."'

On another occasion, Johnny Speight walked in during one of Spike's bawling

'You're awfully thin,' Spike said. 'You've got legs just like Olive Oyl. I wonder who'd want to make love to an elastic band?'

The Goons: (left to right) Harry Secombe, Michael Bentine, Peter Sellers and Spike Milligan in the Graftons pub, 1951 (courtesy Empics)

sessions and said, 'He's not shouting at you, Norma, he's shouting at the world.'

Then came the 'black dog' depressions, when Spike would lock himself in his room, sometimes for days. In the late 1960s and '70s, when his depressions were deeper and longer, he would not emerge for weeks. Norma would slip notes under his door: 'I'm going home now; I'm at the end of the phone if you want me.'

She always made sure she left a little bit of the note out so she could see if he had read them or not. After a time, she would see the notes disappear, only to re-emerge moments later with the message: 'Fuck off and leave me alone' written on them.

'It was then that I'd know he was coming out of it, because he was getting the energy to tell me to bugger off.'

The worst time was when he asked Norma to shoot him. 'His room was boiling hot. It was like walking into India. He had about five of those awful little two-bar electric fires going. The heat was unbearable. He said, "I can't ask anyone else, and I can't do it myself." He had a gun, and he was deadly serious. There was no audience. It was just him and me in this hot, hot room. I said, "No Spike, I can't do that..." He was crying. It was very sad. We talked and talked for hours. I said, "What would it do to your mum? What would happen to your children?"

'Eventually he fell asleep and I went home. A friend said, "Did you never think he would shoot himself once you were gone?" I never did. I felt the time had passed. He'll be alright now, I remember thinking.'

We talk about Spike's close friend Peter Sellers, a man who by all accounts was even more of a monster than Spike. 'Though

'Any chance you could just eat it and not make any fuss? The chef's in one of his moods...'

Peter could be very kind, too,' says Norma. 'When I was going through my divorce he was just sensational. He called me and said, "Oh, Norm! I'm so upset, you're getting a divorce... Spike tells me you're having a bad time..." I said, "Pete, I'm having a terrible time and I don't really want to talk about it." Then Peter said, "Look, I just want to tell you, the first divorce is always the worst."' Norma laughs at the memory. Sellers even offered her the loan of his boat for a few days. 'Take yourself off to Capri,' he told her. 'You'll feel better.'

'That was the good side of Peter. The bad side was horrendous!'

Norma tells the story of Spike's old Austin Cambridge 'Min', a motorcar he was so devoted to he would refer to it as his best friend.

'Peter adored it, too, so Spike said, "Oh, let him have it." Then Sellers had the whole thing re-done, all the leather re-upholstered at great cost,

The worst 'black dog' depression was when Spike asked Norma to shoot him. He said: 'I can't ask anyone else and I can't do it myself'

and gave it back to Spike as a present. The car went back and forth like you'd never believe. I never knew who had it, or where it was! But in the end it remained with Spike.'

That is, until Sellers failed to get an Oscar for his performance in *Being There* (it went instead to Dustin Hoffman for *Kramer v Kramer*).

'All Peter ever wanted was an Oscar, so he was devastated,' explains Norma.

Spike was touring in Australia at the time, and during a live phone link-up between Sellers, Milligan and Irene Handl, Spike jested on-air, 'You didn't get the Oscar then! Ah, Pete, you were caught with your trousers down!'

Peter Sellers was so furious, he sold Spike's beloved car behind his back.

When Spike returned and found out what had happened, Norma, ever the whipping girl, got the blame.

'What else have you given away while I was away?' he ranted. 'My family? Have you given them away? Do I still own a house?'

'He went on and on,' says Norma, 'I said, "For Christ's sake, it's your mate that sold the car, not me!"'

Did the rift last long?

'No. Spike would always forgive Sellers and vice versa. It was a very strange relationship. Very, very close. They could complain about the other to me, but if I ever said anything about either of them, Sellers would say, "Well, you know, he is the genius, the most creative out of all of us."'

Did Norma share this appraisal?

'Oh, yes. Peter once said, "I was just a vase of flowers, and Spike arranged me."

'I thought that was about right. Though I do think Peter would have made it anyway because of his wonderful gift for mimicry. He could be quite frightening. If you sat opposite him for five minutes, he'd take on your persona. Eric [Sykes] didn't like it, and neither did Harry [Secombe]. It was eerie. Eric tells me a story about a mutual friend of theirs who had died a few days earlier. They were in a restaurant when Peter started to impersonate the dead man, and Eric said, "Give over, Peter, it's not the right time..." Peter could just change into a different person. He even started to look like this person.'

O ur conversation steers inevitably back to Spike Milligan. I mention a piece I came across in the *Guardian* describing him as a neo-racist (yet he refused to play to white-only audiences in South Africa).

'Spike was not a racist,' says Norma, emphatically. 'He was concerned about the dangers of uncontrolled immigration... He called it "the beginning of the end." It started when they built the mosque in Regent's Park. Spike said, "I wonder if they'd let me build a Roman Catholic Church in their

Spike with Richard Ingrams, 1994 (courtesy Empics)

country?" I'd say, "Oh, don't start all that again, please! They've got to have somewhere to pray!" Then he'd say, "Well, it's not right... They can come here, of course they can, but they have to accept how we are."

'If someone upset him and he was an Indian, he'd say "bloody Indians". Spike adored Italy, he only ever really ate Italian food. And he loved the Italian people. But one phone call, say, to an Italian telephonist who wouldn't put him through, it would be "those bloody Italians!" He treated everybody the same. People interpreted that as being racist, but he really wasn't.'

Who were Spike's comedy heroes? 'Groucho Marx,' says Norma without hesitation. 'He absolutely adored him. And Buster Keaton. He wasn't keen on Charlie Chaplin. Eric's not either...'

Of the new generation of comedians, Spike, perhaps unsurprisingly, loved the surreally inventive Eddie Izzard.

I wonder what Norma misses the most about Spike?

'Oh, the laughter. And the flowers... Spike was a great flower sender.'

Rather lovely, dearie

TERESA WAUGH *remembers her cousin Rachel de Montmorency –
a woman with a fearsome profile who was full of personality*

It is hardly surprising if, for those who can remember her, Cousin Rachel was always old. Her father fought in the Crimean War, and her brother, René – pronounced 'Rainy' – won a Victoria Cross at Omdurman. She herself had been engaged to Freddie Roberts, son of the famous field marshal of that name, and Freddie, like Rainy, was killed in the Boer War.

A small photograph of Freddie in a little silver frame sat on Rachel's desk to her dying day: narrow face, parting, pencil moustache – just like Rainy. Even in her nineties, she would, before sitting down at her desk, move the photograph a fraction and say, 'Freddie Roberts, dearie.' Occasionally she would add: 'If I could go off the rails now, I would. Oh lor, dearie...'

Upstairs in the Dorset manor house she had built with her sister, Kathleen, in 1914 – 'mock Elizabethan, dearie' – was Kathleen's bedroom. It had remained untouched since her death in the early thirties: a shrine to sibling love.

For a child, Rachel's house held the enchantment of an Aladdin's cave, crowded as it was with sentimental pictures of Jesus among the bluebells, musical boxes, mah jong sets, and every kind of ornament – 'dingbats, dearie' – from Benares brass monkeys and ivory elephants to the delicate prancing china horses that adorned her dining room table. 'We bagged them,' she'd say, as she moved them gently from their allotted places, 'from the Summer Palace.'

Rachel's maternal grandfather, Field Marshal Sir John Michel, had indeed been rewarded for the 'zeal, skill and intrepidity' with which his division burned down the Summer Palace during the Occupation of Peking in 1860, something of which she was very proud.

In the oak-panelled hall hung a chalk drawing of Rachel as a young woman.

> **She treated herself rather as she treated her car, expecting it to go on forever, reluctant to believe its engine was wearing out**

Her hair and eyes were dark, her profile fearsome even then, with a strong, hooked nose, determined chin and thin, set lips. 'I was rather lovely, dearie,' she often said. But my grandfather always used to maintain that 'Freddie Roberts had a demmed lucky escape.'

The name of de Montmorency was adopted by the Irish family of Mount Morris some time during the early years of the 19th century and was, according to *The Complete Peerage*, the biggest cock and bull story ever to be foisted upon the aristocracy. This didn't prevent Rachel from making frequent references to 'our French cousins, dearie'. So, one way and another, she built for herself a quite unnecessary fantasy world of grandeur, developing an equally grand manner to go with it, snorting and waving a dismissive, bejewelled hand in the direction of her long-suffering Switzer Deutch maid whom she addressed in incomprehensible French. Josephine replied in a mixture of pidgin French and excellent English as she helped Madam apply her rouge. 'I was rather lovely, dearie.'

And if anyone dared so much as to smile at Rachel's malapropisms, they were rewarded with a haughty look of such utter contempt that when she announced, with regard to a bothy: 'I'm building a brothel for the gardeners,' not a muscle was seen to move on anyone's face.

What was it that kept Rachel going for so long? Surely not the pre-war Rover with green leather seats that used to boil over on every hill as she drove to the coast for a lobster tea. She would urge it on with a lurch of her body as she gripped the steering wheel, talking to it as if it were an obstinate horse. But perhaps she treated herself rather as she treated the car, expecting it to go on forever, reluctant to believe that its engine was wearing out.

She enjoyed changing her will – malice was not unknown to her – and quarrelling with her relations, rearranging dingbats, saving money, being given things like plums and crab apples, and she enjoyed playing cards – canasta was her game. She played it with unparalleled intensity. Heedless of the tender age of her opponent, she played to win. And not just to win, but to wipe the floor with whatever ten-year-old child she may have happened upon as a playmate. Yet children loved her because she shared so many of their pleasures and their attitudes, and unlike other grown-ups she never tired of their endless prattle. All of these things must have helped to keep her going.

But, above all, Rachel was fearless and, were a marble angel to spread its wings over her grave, it would be the angel of courage for, as she was wont to say: 'We'd better bat on, dearies.'

Swansong
– all aboard for the Oldie cruise

What happens when you put five Oldie contributors and 140 Oldie readers on a luxury cruise ship together? **ROSIE BOYCOTT** *gives us the low-down on the Swan Hellenic Oldie cruise – one of the last ever Swan Hellenic voyages*

It was three years ago that Swan Hellenic first began sponsoring *The Oldie*'s literary lunches at Simpson's-in-the-Strand. We soon realised that it was a mutually rewarding relationship as we are appealing to the same sort of people: SKIers, one and all (spending the kids' inheritance)! It was following one of these lunches that Tony Dyson of Swan Hellenic suggested that we team up for a cruise. There was talk of mounting some kind of stage show but the editor anticipated that this would involve a great deal of effort for an (almost certainly) dreadful result, and proposed instead a simple *Question Time* format, with himself in the role of chairman.

He then approached a number of contributors, and the team, consisting of Mavis Nicholson, Miles Kington, Beryl Bainbridge and me, fell into place. Sadly, as the time for departure approached, Beryl had to go to hospital; Valerie Grove took her place. By the night

of 19th October we were ready. Only Valerie and Trevor had been on a proper cruise before; Richard had crossed the Atlantic in the Queen Mary and rather surprisingly had enjoyed the experience. Would he enjoy a cruise lasting two weeks? We were about to find out.

We knew from the outset that we were going to be in fine company, as there had been an overwhelming response from readers

We knew from the outset that we were going to be in fine company, as there had been an overwhelming response from our readers when the cruise was advertised in *The Oldie*. Swan Hellenic had been expecting about fifty to sign up. In the event, 140 of you decided to set sail with us from Barcelona.

Early on Saturday 21st October, we flew in a Qantas charter to Barcelona. The passengers eyed each other up, confident that among the mix would be at least one with whom they would discover a connection. We were whisked aboard the Minerva II within 58 minutes of the plane touching down, which, everyone agreed, was extraordinarily impressive, particularly after the miserably long queue we'd all endured at Terminal Four at the crack of dawn. Now, here we were in the sun, on board, being served drinks from the Wheeler Bar, enjoying splendid views of the city.

Swan Hellenic goes to great lengths to organise excursions at the various ports of call, but inevitably some passengers choose to take matters into their own hands and break away from the herd! One such instance occurred early on. Mavis, Richard and Maureen Lipman (the onboard star cabaret act) set off to see the famous Gaudi Cathedral, the Sagrada Familia. Deciding to spurn the official tour, they boarded a local bus, having been assured by Trevor Grove that it would take them directly to the front doors of the cathedral. After travelling for at least half an hour, deep in a discussion about the Catalan question, they realised they were heading rapidly out of town. At the next stop they made a rapid exit (not having paid the fare) and hailed a taxi to return to the city. They so entranced the sympathetic driver with tales of their plight that he let them off with a half fare.

Malta was the next stop, where we sailed into the magnificent Grand Harbour at midday. The sun blazed down as it did throughout the voyage, and we were all surprised by how much there was to do on those 'days at sea'. Lectures, painting classes (much favoured by Mavis and Maureen), the spa (much favoured by me and many Oldie readers), which offered slimming treatments, facials, pedicures, massage, Pilates, keep-fit with Emma – we went in for them all. (The average weight gain on an SH cruise is 2.2 pounds and some of us were determined not to succumb.) We also played ping-pong and, of course, made lots of new friends.

In between mouthfuls of kedgeree and kippers, smoked tuna, crème brûlée, crustless cucumber sandwiches and freshly baked scones, we met a varied and wonderful cast of new friends. In the evenings we were entertained by Bobbie Winchester at her piano, and one night the editor sat down at the keyboard and led us in a rousing singsong which included a full-throttle rendition of 'Rule Britannia'. Maureen brought the house down not once, but twice in two hour-long one-woman shows. On the last night, we crammed onto the dance

A sudden lurch of the boat threw me into his arms. 'Oh, she is frisky tonight,' he said with a beam

floor in the Orpheus Bar and bopped around to the music of the Marines' Band. It was the only night in the entire two weeks when the sea was ever so slightly rough. As I was dancing with Hugh Leslie, cruise director of Swan Hellenic for the last 14 years, a sudden lurch threw me (almost) into his arms. 'Oh, she is frisky tonight,' he said with a beam. I hasten to add that he was referring here to our splendid ship on which we all felt so much at home.

I could go on... and on... suffice to say that Oldie readers turned out to be just as terrific as we hoped and Swan Hellenic is clearly a perfect partner. But as we left the ship on a slightly overcast Madeira afternoon, Minerva II was bound for South America, the Caribbean, New Orleans and the Amazon, before crossing to the Pacific through the Panama Canal and rounding Cape Horn on her final journey to Cadiz, where the anchor will be lowered for the last time on 7th April.

The company's original 1950s idea was simple and brilliant: if you wanted to study and experience the classical worlds, team up a group of students with a group of experts and put them on a ship travelling round the Aegean. The imposition of the £500 limit in the Sixties boosted the business yet further and SH

Left: Maureen enjoying her serenade
Above: Rosie and the Ed in Libya
Below: Mavis and Gaddafi strike a pose

sailed into an increasingly successful future. News of the company's impending demise brought sadness and anger to many, particularly members of the long-serving crew and regular lecturers and entertainers on board.

Good news

Since this article appeared in *The Oldie*, the plight of Swan Hellenic has changed dramatically. Under chairman Lord Sterling, and new owner All Leisure Group PLC, the Voyages of Discovery will return on 28 May 2008 onboard no other than SH's former old favourite, the 350-berth, country-house style *Minerva 1*.

Visit www.swanhellenic.com for the 2008/2009 itinerary.

'To be honest, it's no worse than Scunthorpe on a Saturday night'

I once met...

Harold Wilson

This impromptu meeting took place in a men's lavatory in the bowels of the Waldstadion, Frankfurt. It was June 1974; West Germany were the host country, and Brazil and Scotland were meeting in an early World Cup final match. I made my way down from the press box at half time with no goals on the scoreboard to find some bits and pieces for a World Cup diary. In the process, I made for the nearest male convenience and found myself in the company of a small, chubby man smoking a cigar and reeking of brandy fumes. He had to clutch the toilet to remain upright. He began to go on about how unlucky England had been not to score against the World Cup holders. I thought it unkind to inform the Prime Minister of the United Kingdom, Harold Wilson, that Scotland were Brazil's

I found myself in the company of a small, chubby man smoking a cigar and reeking of brandy fumes

opponents, and that England had not even qualified for the finals. 'If I were manager I would change their formation and go back to the days of inside rights and inside lefts like Clem Stephenson.' After those words of wisdom, the Prime Minister bade me farewell and tottered out to be met by a waiting minder. A mass of incoming Jocks wearing tam-o'-shanters should have reminded him that he was in the company of a foreign army known as Tartan.

Wilson had arrived by helicopter with the German Chancellor, Willy Brandt, and they must have enjoyed a very long lunch. It was a difficult time for Wilson, who had only recently regained the Premiership from Ted Heath and reluctantly taken charge of a country plagued by strikes, trade union problems and a general sense of dissatisfaction. He was drinking a lot of brandy and was under the bullying thumb of his political secretary, Marcia Williams (later Baroness Falkender).

This World Cup match offered Wilson a chance to relax for once and he jumped at it. Back in the press box, I told that doyen of football writers, Geoffrey Green, Association Football correspondent for the *Times*, about the Prime Minister's muddle. 'Well, dear boy', he laughed against himself, 'I have woken up in the past forgetting who was playing, and had to be reminded of the name of the teams.'

This reminded me of a story Sir Bobby Robson, then the manager of Ipswich, had told me about Geoffrey's friend, Johnny Cobbold, entering the team's

dressing room at Filbert Street, Leicester, and warmly congratulating the team on their brilliant performance and exciting goals. Ipswich had been mauled rotten, and Robson had to remind his chairman that, 'We were wearing our white strip away shirts today, Mr Chairman.'

And Clem Stephenson? 'Stephenson,' Green added, 'won two FA Cup winners' medals with Aston Villa in 1913 and 1920, and another with Huddersfield two years later. He was still playing for them in 1928 when I went to a Wembley final for the first time. Clem was a great favourite with the

Huddersfield crowd, and Harold Wilson a young man among them.'

The Scotland v. Brazil match remained goalless, though Scotland would have won had not their captain, Billy Bremner, missed a sitter. It cost Scotland a place in the next round, but they remained unbeaten.

Harold Wilson gave an impromptu press conference later, which I attended. He had visibly sobered up and dusted himself down. After the usual political questions about his meeting with Brandt, he moved onto the match, now aware that our representatives were Scotland. Then he suddenly accused their manager, the unfortunate Willie Ormond, of using the wrong tactics. 'I would have used Lorimer at inside left like Clem Stephenson,' he intoned. 'The Scottish team would have done far better.'

As if Ormond didn't have enough to worry about. Inside forwards were very much in a past that included his own distinguished career with Hibernian. His squad had given him some nightmares before the World Cup with that wee Celtic wizard, Jimmy Johnstone, who was found drifting off the Ayrshire coast in a beautiful pea-green boat. Now they had to beat Yugoslavia in the next match, which they failed to do.

The Prime Minister, meanwhile, returned to Downing Street without waiting to watch the final in Munich at which West Germany beat Holland. He would remain Prime Minister for under two years before hanging up his boots. Free of strikes and Marcia Williams, he could put his feet up in his Scilly Islands summer retreat and dream over a large glass of brandy of the days when Clem Stephenson wiggled and dribbled in the cause of Harold's beloved town. Sheer magic, Clem.

JOHN MOYNIHAN

'I'm bitter. At what stage do I become twisted as well?'

The world according to
Enfield Snr
Gardening with guns

FIRST things first – I must try to make my peace with Alice Pitman, whom I have upset by suggesting that she was more keen on Tesco than is entirely proper. I recant at once. I am sure she has a clear perception of the evil ways of that baleful organisation. Also, I do not want to be on the wrong side of one who writes with such wit and elegance, and, furthermore, she is very pretty, which is another reason for trying to scramble back into her good books. Whether such a sexist remark will make things better or worse between us, I shall, in due course, discover.

Having mended my fences with Shopping (or not, as the case may be), I hope I do not now tread on the toes of Gardening by venturing onto the patch that properly belongs to David Wheeler, but I wish to devote this column to my War on Wildlife in the garden. I am full of inspiration at the moment, having spent the summer breathing out threats and slaughter like St Paul in his pre-Damascus days. The death toll so far is two rats, three magpies, seven rabbits, six squirrels and a quantity of mice. Others of the enemy are lurking in the undergrowth, and I am expecting the body count to rise further.

Now, in explanation, I shoot the rabbits because they eat things in the garden, and I put the corpses in the magpie trap. If I catch a magpie, I do it to death in the belief that this is a kindness to the songbirds, as dead magpies cannot eat their chicks, which they otherwise most certainly would.

I am slightly sorry about the mice, though. They do annoying things, like eating holes in the potato sacks, but I am not really out to get them. They are, as it were, civilians caught in the crossfire of battle, as they persist in immolating themselves upon the trap I set for the rats. Your average rat, of course, is a cunning fellow. He comes by night to eat the chicken food and Master Rat is too fly to eat your poison when there is chicken food on offer. I thought I had found his Achilles heel when I discovered that he

has a weakness for peanut butter, so I baited the spring trap and the walk-in trap with this and caught the two rats above mentioned, but since then they have passed the word around that peanut butter is dangerous stuff and I have caught no more, only mice.

In this the rats are smarter than the squirrels. Squirrel psychology is an interesting matter, as they are clever enough to solve the most intricate puzzles to get at food, and yet are also extremely stupid.

I looked out of the bathroom window to see two squirrels eating corn meant for the birds, so I got my gun and shot one. The other ran off, but by the time I was dressed, it was back, feeding beside the corpse of its departed friend, and got shot in turn. If they were as bright as rats, they would have long since worked out that the Enfield garden is no place for a squirrel in daylight hours.

Squirrels are not the cuddly friendly creatures that they appear. If you let

> *I looked out to see two squirrels eating corn meant for the birds, so I got my gun and shot one*

them, they wreck the whole strawberry crop by ripping the green fruits off the plants and chucking them around. Also, last year they began to eat the apple trees by tearing chunks off the trunks and branches. They can be caught in the walk-in trap, because they have the same liking for peanut butter as the rats, but I have given this up as I kept catching a hedgehog.

A squirrel in a trap gnashes its yellow fangs, chatters and rattles the bars, but the hedgehog sits quietly waiting for me to let him out. I think he is in a state of tranquil euphoria brought on by the peanut butter, safe in the knowledge that he and I are on the same side in this war, as he is an enemy to slugs.

Apart from any dealings I may have with hedgehogs, gardening seems to be like fishing. It is supposed to be the contemplative man's recreation, and is actually a pretty sanguinary business.

Closet encounters

Australian actor **TRADER FAULKNER** *met John Gielgud, Esmé Percy and Noël Coward in the Fifties – all of whom took rather a shine to him...*

I had auditioned for John Gielgud. A replacement was required for Richard Burton in Christopher Fry's *The Lady's Not For Burning*, since Burton was off to Stratford to play Henry V. I had just arrived from Sydney with a recommendation from Tyrone Guthrie, and at the end of the final audition I was told to wait on stage. Presently a tall bald man sauntered down the aisle and addressed me from the stalls.

'I'm John Gielgud. What's your name?'

'Ronald Faulkner, sir.'

'Oh God! What a dreary name.'

'Well, down under, I'm also known as Trader.'

'Trader? T R A D E R!!' Spoken more beautifully than I've ever heard it uttered since, like a basso profundo rhinoceros yawning. 'What a wonderful name! We'll bill you on Broadway as Trader. Welcome to the company.'

At an early rehearsal, everything I did was wrong. Then, suddenly, I did something correctly: 'Yes, dear Trader, yes,' Gielgud said. He was very impulsive and had a barbed wit, of which I was often the victim. Early in rehearsal, a flat Australian vowel must have crept into my dialogue, because a yell came from Gielgud in the stalls: 'Oh Trader, for God's sake take that compost out of your vowel sounds.' He sent me round the theatre block repeating dreary vowel exercises such as: 'Brown's cows go round and round the town house.' But on this occasion, when I had got some piece of his direction correct, he rushed over impulsively and ran his hand through my thick head of Aussie hair. Having

Gielgud impulsively ran a hand through my hair. 'Oh, forgive me, I mustn't do that, I'm a poof'

realised what he had done, he backed away very quickly and said: 'Oh, forgive me, I mustn't do that, I'm a poof!'

Gielgud was such a gentleman of the old school that no-one could take offence: he would often show off like a child. As the new boy in the company and the youngest, my grooming as a West End actor came at a price. Although Gielgud may have been effeminate, he was never vicious, at least not to me. Apart from being on Christian name terms, his behaviour was very formal, except when impulse got the better of him. All this was at a time before homosexuality became legal, though it was tacitly accepted socially. At Christmas in 1950, Gielgud gave every member of the company a present. His gift to me was a fur-lined Christian Dior leopard-skin jockstrap, and it kept me cosy on many a subsequent winter night.

In the early days most of the London cast were very snooty towards me, an untried Aussie, replacing their illustrious colleague.

I was seldom invited out for a drink after the show as the others were either married or had

their own pursuits. But one member of the cast did befriend me – the kind and very old Esmé Percy. He had acted with Sarah Bernhardt, and I came to realise just how Bernhardt must have acted, sounded and moved. All of five feet tall in high-heeled boots, with strands of what remained of a once fine head of hair, he wore a black eye-patch – he was minus one eye because his faithful dog had jumped up to lick his nose and removed his eye instead – but they were still the best of friends. He looked exactly like Rumplestiltskin. He sported a cane with an ivory handle, a gift from the 'divine Sarah' who had once used it in a play, and a red cloak.

On that memorable Christmas Eve of 1950, I went to dinner in New York (the play had now transferred to Broadway) with 'Rumpledforeskin'. He told me he was madly in love, absolutely revitalised at 87 after meeting a very shy lady called Dorothy: would I come along as a third party to make the evening more relaxed? – and 'Darling heart, you will, I know, charm her and make it a memorable evening.'

How prescient Esmé was! He had booked a table for three at an elegant restaurant in Greenwich Village. As the minutes ticked by I kept wondering how, or rather with whom, could this old fellow possibly be in love? Was she some besotted elderly fan from his early days, one who had seen him in his glorious youth, followed his career, and was making a date to see him again after God knows how many years? I was expecting at any moment to see an antiquated version of Isadora Duncan totter through the door.

Our table was in the centre of a vast barn of a room. Esmé ordered champagne. I sipped, he drank in large gulps. A second bottle was ordered. I felt he was being stood up. How wrong I was. He started to become histrionic and began to declaim. 'Who has known love...? Love that can begin as a tiny bud... the flicker of an eyelid... a shy glance.' Tables all round us began to fall silent, and the entire dining-room was his audience. He took up his full glass of champagne, invoked the divine Sarah and then... 'What it is to feel love's passion in my decline. The object of my passion, the flower of my ecstasy about to bloom, my darling, is you!' He toasted me, drank the entire glass and collapsed in his chair.

Suddenly the restaurant was bedlam. A waiter came over and shouted at me: 'You goddam fairy, get out of here and take that decrepit faggot with you!' I tried to lower my voice an octave and shouted 'I am not a poofter!'

'Then what are you doing with that senile faggot? This is a respectable eating house, so get out of here, goddam you!'

By now there was a chorus of diners shouting 'Goddam fairy, get out of here.'

I remember dragging the old, very drunk man into a taxi. 'Driver,' he yelled, 'take us to the Hudson River Bridge, I'm going to throw myself off, my love is destroying me.'

At the next evening performance the old fellow wouldn't speak to me, and I felt it would be more tactful to leave him alone.

Esmé's new lover was an obnoxious and effeminate parasite who latched onto him and took him for all he was worth.

I met them once in Fifth Avenue. That was the last I heard of Esmé, who must have died soon after.

I remember him as an ultra-sensitive, extravagant, theatrical personality of an age that is long gone. He was one of the gentlest, kindest men I ever knew. Part of

his tragedy was living in an age of sexual intolerance. He wouldn't have harmed a fly.

During the 1955 season at Stratford-on-Avon I was staying with Laurence Olivier and Vivien Leigh at Notley Abbey in Buckinghamshire. We had all driven down after the evening performance of *Macbeth* starring Larry and Vivien. Noël Coward had attended the performance, and we all had dinner and magnificent wines afterwards. I wasn't feeling very confident at a table full of sparkling guests. The wines elicited dazzling conversation; Coward juggled his notorious witticisms with consummate ease until we all reeled off to bed.

The other guests had their breakfast in bed – but, excited to be there, I went downstairs. After I had collected my food, in glided England's 'talent to amuse' in an elegant dressing gown, smoking a de Reszke cigarette and exhaling perfectly shaped smoke rings. He floated over and offered me a winning smile.

'I thought you were very good as Malcolm last night, dear boy. You have a promising future.'

'Thank you, Mr Coward.'

He leaned towards me, exuding a strong odour of Mitsouko.

'Tell me, dear boy, is your bum available this morning?'

'No, Mr Coward, not this morning or any other. I'm a poker not a poofter.'

'What a tragedy!' said the master. 'Life is full of disappointment, but we must soldier on. Would you pass the marmalade?'

Far left: Trader Faulkner in his glorious youth Left: John Gielgud

BILL PROUD

'I was possessed by the devil once'

Esmé said 'Driver, take us to the Hudson River Bridge, I'm going to throw myself off, my love is destroying me'

Left: Noël Coward

An ill wind blows

PIERS BRENDON *finds Holocaust-denying David Irving an absurd figure – but is the decision to lock him up any less ridiculous?*

JOHN KENT

I first met David Irving about twenty years ago at a television studio in Birmingham. He was being quizzed about his cock-eyed theory that during the war Winston Churchill got warnings from the Bletchley Park code-breakers about German air raids so that he could flee from London when they were imminent. I was one of Irving's interrogators and I found no difficulty in exposing the absurdity of his suggestion that Churchill was too cowardly to face the bombing – 'London could take it; he could not.'

Courage was, of course, Churchill's transcendent virtue. So I simply provided a catalogue of outstanding instances: his riding a white pony within range of Afghan marksmen in the hope of winning a medal; his preferring to be in the trenches on the Western Front, where the whisky flowed freely, rather than staying dry behind the lines; his urchin enjoyment of the bangs made by high explosives; his cheering up when the doodlebugs again injected an element of danger into World War II. Irving's claim was in tatters but he himself was not a bit abashed.

Nor did he appear to resent the criticism. On the contrary, since we were lodged at the same hotel, he kept me up late in a friendly discussion. I found him charming, though I did detect a

slightly crazed look in his eye as well as more than a hint of menace and malice. For example, he invariably mentioned that this or that person was Jewish, whether or not it had anything to do with the case. In fact, Irving reminded me of a Gauleiter who might be extremely nice to your dog before ordering your grandmother to be shot in the back of the neck.

What amazed me, though, was his encyclopaedic ignorance of printed sources. He adored manuscripts but

Irving reminded me of a Gauleiter who might be extremely nice to your dog before ordering your grandmother to be shot

disregarded books. Despite writing a vast tome about Churchill, Irving had not even read Roy Foster's seminal biography of Winston's father, Lord Randolph. Nor did he seem to know any history before the 20th century. So *Churchill's War* is full of incidental howlers, such as the statement that William Pitt was Prime Minister 'at the time of Waterloo'.

I was vouchsafed a more recent

insight into Irving's methods when he came to the Churchill Archives Centre in Cambridge, where I was Keeper, to read the diary of Sir Alexander Cadogan, head of the Foreign Office during the war. In great excitement Irving told me that he had discovered that Britain knew about the Japanese intention to attack Pearl Harbor. The proof lay in Cadogan's entry for 7 December 1941, which opened with the words: 'A lovely morning but an ominously strong NW wind.' This apparently indicated that Cadogan knew of the 'WINDS-EXECUTE' message broadcast by Japan to warn its ambassadors that war was imminent.

I expressed total scepticism. Did not Cadogan often begin his diary with a weather report, sensibly omitted in the published version? What was the wind doing? (It was blowing a force '3 to 4' north-westerly.) How could this ludicrously circumstantial snippet controvert the mass of evidence indicating that the bombing of Pearl Harbor came as a complete surprise in London as well as Washington? Irving listened but he was not convinced. In

'Ignore him, he's after scraps'

the second volume of *Churchill's War* he printed his own version of the story, including a facsimile of the entry in Cadogan's diary.

This 'discovery' is about as intellectually contemptible as Irving's case for the denying of the Holocaust, which has earned him a three-year gaol sentence in Austria. But to take his claim seriously is to suggest that Irving is something more than a crackpot. And to imprison him for making it not only risks turning him into a famous martyr, it implies that the case for the reality of the Holocaust is weak since it has to be sustained by law.

Moreover, if you lock up historians for getting things wrong they would all be behind bars and there would be no room for anyone else.

The Irving case is one sign among many that the world is succumbing to a new epidemic of fundamentalism. So liberals should stand up and be counted. They should oppose the government's current attempt to outlaw the 'glorification' of terrorism, something which it cannot define. They should defend free speech, especially when they abhor what is being said.

Despite his fascist views, David Irving himself is not a complete stranger to tolerance. Reviewing one of his books, which was more ill-written than usual, I said that it seemed to have been badly translated from the Lithuanian. Far from taking offence, he sent me a comic postcard saying that he was impressed by my command of that language.

When I clap my hands I want you to perform an emergency stop

TEST

HUNTER

I once met...
Queen Mary

POPPERFOTO/ALAMY

THE EXACT date escapes me, but it was in the late spring or early summer of 1941, and I was stationed in the area of Savernake Forest. I had been mended, restored and re-equipped following the Continental adventure of the previous year, and was awaiting posting to a new unit.

The weather was fine, sunny with a slight breeze, as I set out one afternoon to walk the two miles or so into Marlborough. As I ambled along, enjoying the afternoon, a large black car passed me and drew into the side of the road. A chauffeur alighted, walked back to me, saluted and said 'Her Majesty Queen Mary would like to give you a lift, Sir.'

Rather in a daze, I walked to the car and, indeed, there in the car was Queen Mary, unmistakeable in her toque with her high-necked dress and a band around her neck. I climbed into the car and sat. The car moved off. There was a short silence and then she uttered, 'What is your name?' I told her. Another short

silence. 'What is your regiment?' This information given she said, 'Good, good'.

We drove on a little further. 'Do you write to your mother every week?' she demanded. 'I certainly try to ma'am.' 'Good, good,' she said.

Shortly we reached the centre of Marlborough. The car stopped, the

In a daze, I walked to the car and there was Queen Mary, unmistakeable

chauffeur opened the door. I alighted, said, 'Thank you for the lift, ma'am', and gave her my smartest salute. 'Good luck to you,' she said and drove off, leaving a rather bemused young soldier wondering who would believe him when he told the story in the mess. I discovered later that I was by no means the only one to be picked up by Queen Mary.

LEO MORRIS

The word 'banjo' is my favourite word. The sound of a banjo is my favourite sound. The shape of a banjo is my favourite shape. I like banjos more than I like myself.

I play the banjo quite well considering I've only been playing for three years. It is not an easy instrument to master – but then again, I am sure learning to play the triangle is not as easy as it looks. Such is my devotion to the instrument that my friends have taken to calling me 'Banjo-Andy', which is really an insult wrapped up in an affectionate nickname. But I'd rather be 'Banjo-Andy' than 'Triangle-Andy'.

I have been surrounded by very supportive people my whole life. But when I started playing the banjo all of this came to a sudden end. My friends and family all smiled and pretended they loved the banjo, but secretly they were planning my death.

So, I decided to go to a place where banjos and banjo players are accepted. Not just accepted but revered. A magical place of mythical inbred mountain men and chewing tobacco. A place where it is not a sign of madness to wear a cowboy hat and cowboy boots at the age of eighty. A place I had dreamed of all my banjo-playing life: the Southern states of Tennessee, North Carolina and Kentucky.

I arrived at Banjocamp, Tennessee, in autumn 2004. It is a banjo-improvement camp held annually in the beautiful county of Dickson, an hour outside of Nashville. On my arrival the other students welcomed me as a conquering hero. I felt like a famous general returning from battle with the bloody spoils of war. I wish their joy could have been attributed to my legendary banjo-playing skills but, alas, it was my Scottish accent and pale complexion.

I was getting irritated with my camp-mates – lovely people who all play the banjo better than you do slowly lose their loveliness

There was the assumption that if I had travelled so far to be there, then I must be one heck of a banjo player, which I sort of thought I was. We were all in for a shocking disappointment.

Those euphoric, adrenalin-fuelled first hours were bliss. We all showed each

Those banjo blues

*Cartoonist and banjo player, **ANDY MCKAY**, thought he was a pretty good musician – until he travelled to the Deep South of America and enrolled at 'Banjocamp'...*

other our banjos and exchanged banjo stories. My banjo was the crappiest banjo in the camp, which was a slight blow, but I knew some of them were just 'showboating' – hoping a fancy piece of hardware would be some sort of substitute for talent. I was wrong. Very, very wrong. They all played like angels. I was the crappiest banjo player with the crappiest banjo.

It became apparent that being Scottish was my only saving grace. If I had been from Alabama or North Carolina and had dared to play the Beverly Hillbillies theme tune as badly as I did, I would have been lynched. But I wasn't going to give up. With my new friends' support I would leave this place a better, more confident banjo player.

My spirits lifted when I discovered I had been placed in the beginners group. 'I have everything to gain,' I thought.

Well, whatever standard 'beginner' is in Tennessee, I hadn't yet reached it. I was a pre-beginner whose popularity

was starting to dwindle. My hot licks (small, fancy pieces of banjo playing) were cooler than a frozen pizza. My understanding of chord positions was on a par with a two-year-old's knowledge of quantum physics. My technical precision was borderline offensive. I was becoming concerned my banjo might be used as firewood at the campfire sing-along.

Thankfully, there was one person at Banjocamp who had no interest in playing the banjo. Johnny, camp leader and living banjo legend, preferred telling tales of his wild-man past, and as I was the only other person in the room who couldn't give a stuff about playing the banjo, I sat down and listened to his life.

'Me and my brother had just finished a show in Birmingham, Alabama,' he rumbled. 'I was taking my banjer off to take a bow but didn't see the low ceiling fan above me and WHAP! Goddam thing cut the banjer head clean off!'

'That's terrible,' I said.

'I was madder than a bear up a tree! I'll tell yer Andy, it cost me a pretty penny to get it fixed.'

He had started to get agitated. I could see that the telling of this story was a painful one. To a musician, an instrument is like a child. I cannot imagine what a parent would go through if their child got its head cut off by a ceiling fan.

He composed himself and continued. 'Two months later we was back at the same auditorium. Goddam it, if the same thing doesn't go and happen again!' he exclaimed, his voice becoming more and more emotionally charged. 'I lift the banjer over my head and WHAP! – the fan cuts the new head off!'

'My God,' I gasped. 'You must have been so upset.'

'I was reeeeal mad, Andy! I took out my pistol and shot that mother till it stopped moving. The crowd was yellin' so loud it sounded like rain on a tin roof.'

In the South, it is not unusual for a person to own a gun. It is unusual, however, for that person to open fire on a ceiling fan.

By day two I was getting irritated with my camp-mates. Lovely people who all play the banjo better than you do slowly lose their loveliness. I tried to swallow

'Penny for your thoughts dear'

my pride, however, and attempted to learn something from this vast ocean of banjo knowledge. I tried to copy what I was seeing, but it was just a flesh-toned

I cannot imagine what a parent would go through if their child got its head cut off by a ceiling fan

blur of hands passing up and down the fret board. I was out of my depth and decided to throw in the towel. I wasn't about to let virtuoso banjo playing spoil a perfectly good trip to the countryside.

I crab-crawled my way out the rear exit of the tuition hall, and made for the kitchen. 'Might as well be first in the dinner queue,' I thought. Three hours first to be exact, but at least the silence of the dining room was preferable to the hellish noise of fifty banjos being played beautifully.

The kitchen lady didn't speak a word of English, which made asking for a chicken and sweetcorn sandwich difficult. In the end she gave me a fried chicken drumstick, which wasn't what I wanted, but it was still better than the humiliation of the tuition hall.

This was not what I had imagined for myself when I left home. My banjo fantasies would remain unfulfilled until I became a better banjo player. 'But surely one can be a "successful" banjo player without being the "best" banjo player?' I mused. 'Maybe I should take the banjo in a different musical direction? Maybe I should pioneer a new style of music (to distract people from the fact that I am not that good a banjo player)? Maybe I should invent bluegrass-reggae, or "bleggae" if you will, and I can be the best, and only, bleggae player in the world?' Or maybe I should take up the triangle.

'Hi – I'm in a two-minute silence...'

Living with the Mole money

SUE TOWNSEND, *creator of the famous secret diarist Adrian Mole, speaks to* **MAVIS NICHOLSON** *about her own secret writing, her playwright roots, and how to avoid becoming unpleasantly rich...*

Sue Townsend arrived at the June Oldie Lunch in a crisp white trouser-suit and a wheelchair. Sue is also registered blind. But her humorous, matter-of-fact attitude stops you fussing over her.

She didn't give a speech, but took questions, the first of which was from Richard Ingrams who wondered why she insisted on living in Leicester.

'Since I was born in Leicester, grew up in Leicester, married in Leicester, had my children in Leicester, and my extended family live in Leicester, and since Leicester is an hour and ten minutes from London, I thought I'd be mad to leave. There was no reason to move.'

A question from the floor: 'At the time you started on Adrian Mole, was one of your sons the same age?'

'No. But my eldest son is now forty, and his life has been blighted by people assuming he is Adrian Mole. When he was doing a degree course in English, a lecturer started talking about my writing and he never let on I was his Mum.

'I wrote Adrian Mole in my secret writing years. I was a secret writer for twenty years. My first husband didn't know.

'I wrote when the children were in bed. I'd start at midnight so I could completely concentrate. When you have children they are always, always with you.

'I suppose all my children have suffered in small ways, but they also moved into a bigger house and had foreign holidays for the first time – thanks to Adrian Mole – and we call it the Mole money. "Oh! Mole will pay," we say. "He'll get it for us."'

Why did she start to be a secret writer? someone asked. 'I think readers often spill over into being writers. The two go together. Since I was eight years old I have been a reader, and to a certain extent that was all I did. I had a fabulous English teacher as well.

'I was up for a prize for best essay but I didn't get it because I had used a cliché: I compared the clouds to cotton-wool balls. That was a good lesson because I have avoided them since.

'It was only when I married my second husband that I confessed to being a writer. After I had told him, he saw an advertisement for a writers' workshop at the Phoenix Theatre, so I joined. After six weeks one of the directors came up to me and said I should try to write a play. I hadn't written or spoken a word since I got there. I didn't know where to begin. I wrote one called *Wish Fulfilment,* about women in a waiting room. One woman who had cancer did a dance on a table in her corset using her false teeth as castanets; and a couple who were not making love properly who were taught how to in a cubicle. Without telling me, he entered it in a Thames Television thing and I was asked to go up there.'

Sue tottered up to London in high heels and proper clothes that she borrowed from her mother. She walked into a room and there were John Mortimer and Michael Billington, and she was told to talk about her play:

'I didn't know where to start and then John Mortimer rescued me and read chunks from it and made them all laugh. He's a lovely man who has done endless good work for new writers in the theatre. When I got home there was a telegram saying I had won. I then became resident writer at the Phoenix Theatre.

'The play that sold out was one I wrote about the redevelopment of Leicester and how the developers completely destroyed our city. It brought in people who had never been to the theatre before, my extended family included.'

Lunch over, Sue and her daughter Liz and I went off to talk. I asked her which was the most expensive pair of shoes she'd ever bought. She practically blushed when she told us. They were boots and the shop had told her Cher had bought a pair. '£500! That's a month's rent for some people.'

But she has never been lavish in her lifestyle. 'I gave loads of money away. To individuals and causes and charities. I had to. It would have isolated me from things that matter to me. And things I wrote about. I can't imagine why people

buy big country houses and have round-the-clock guard dogs and electronic gates. I don't like the very rich.' We started grumbling that you never hear people caring about socialism these days. Sue said she believed in socialism even more, as capitalism had failed to make people happy. 'Unbridled capitalism is going to result in everybody being made more miserable,' she said. 'Goods are getting cheaper, but I don't remember

My eldest son is now forty and his life has been blighted by people assuming that he is Adrian Mole

people ever asking for cheap food. The word socialism has been deliberately discredited. I do really believe in sharing. It seems so completely fair and the only way to live. People are acquiring more and more objects, and as soon as they get them home the thrill has gone.

'And then I have been noticing how a lot of young people don't seem to have a very ready vocabulary. In the last *Big Brother*, a lad called Glyn from Wales was in the swimming pool and as he got out he said that he couldn't swim in water that was timid. Another contestant told him "Timid means shy. I think you mean tepid." And I heard a Winter Olympics contestant say about winning a bronze: "I wasn't too dis-happy."'

What's happened to passionate political views from young people?

'There is a terrible cynicism. And a laziness of not thinking things through and not having alternatives. I don't

know any children that debate the big questions. They are not taught the same way at school. We had debates in my girls' grammar school. Such as whether it was better to work or be a housewife.'

Which reminded me. Why didn't Sue write about Adrianna Mole?

'Because men keep most of their feelings hidden and I wanted to keep it a secret diary.'

Sue had referred to watching the telly. How much could she actually see?

'I can't see out of one eye at all. I can see shapes and light out of the other. I can tell when it is bright. But I can't see expressions on faces. I am dependent on the expression in the voice now. I have always had a very good visual memory. I have sixty years' worth of clear snapshots to bring up when I want to.'

Since she can't read, can she listen to books in the same way?

'No, and they are often slashed to pieces. I listen to talk radio and that's how I keep up to date with what people are thinking. And now I listen to music, I used to only play Tchaikovsky's Violin Concerto in D over and over again when I was working through the night.'

I didn't want to part from Sue Townsend – she's lovely and funny and you feel warmed in her company. I went off laughing to myself, remembering when we were in the Ladies together before a *Woman's Own* lunch. Sue was rubbing some stuff under her eyes from a tube. I asked her what it was. 'Haemorrhoid ointment,' she said. 'To bring down the swelling under my eyes. Want some?'

JUNE AND GERALD by NAF

My brother's been taken into hospital.

That's terrible, June, I'm really sorry.

Is it a mental hospital or a normal hospital?

From troubles to treats

While others bemoan the state of the NHS, **RABBI LIONEL BLUE** *says that he has often found hospitals rather pleasant and uplifting places to be. Can it be true?*

Generally speaking I've had a good experience of hospitals. And this is just as well, as having recently turned 75, I shall certainly be spending more time in them. I owe this attitude partly to my mother, who had been a bubbly flapper in the twenties and taught me early on how to turn troubles into treats.

Even in her nineties she couldn't be bothered with barley water, baby wipes and such. What she needed, she told me, was a monster-size bottle of Charlie perfume to fascinate the specialist and his train of young doctor disciples. They all liked her because she didn't mind being prodded, questioned and examined. (She often gave the game away, revealing in stage whispers what was really wrong with her, to help them get the right answers.)

I also owe a lot to two old ladies, normally marooned in their high-rise tower blocks, who once a month were taken to the clinic by a special bus. These visits were the high points of their lives. Their pensions couldn't stretch to sandwiches in the canteen, so they made their own and filled a thermos and treated the waiting room like the foyer of a five-star hotel. And when their numbers and names were called out, they swept off to the inner sanctum, proud to be singled out so publicly. From them I learnt that waiting was an

integral part of hospital life and it should be provided for. So if I've got time I pick and mix my own picnic bag with a half pound of my favourite chocolate, baby wipes, a thermos of sweet tea, a notebook if I want to work, and a long book with an assured happy ending if I don't. I like learning a language while waiting, so I take a grammar too.

I also learnt from my two OAPs how to get a modicum of fun from my treatment. I noticed, for example, that when the tube to which I was attached was depressed, I could watch my ruby red lifeblood flowing out of me, and when it was lifted, it all flowed back into me again. Watching this happen entertained me far more than TV and superior cultural delights. It also cured me of my mild phobia about blood. I got great pleasure out of that drip.

Another curiosity caused me a lot of wonderment and laughter. Whenever

I had to change cubicles, I always got to eat what the previous occupant had ordered the day before. Now, some people have very bizarre preferences and strange ideas about what goes with what – cold tomato pilchards with hot cabbage, for example! It was almost as odd as my mother's favourite: fried kippers with strawberry jam.

But enough of food that makes me queasy. What about vegetable samosas instead? They were not on the hospital menu but were given me by the patient in the next bed, whose wife had made them lovingly for him. He was a kind man, and after one look at me decided I needed strengthening. I've always been impressed in hospitals at the way sick patients minister to each other. I learnt this after being brought to hospital unexpectedly by ambulance. During a period of acute stress, I had

my first full epileptic attack. I remember looking at some grotesque masks in the windows of a joke shop to cheer myself up. I later learnt from people who were there that I went rigid and purple and crashed onto the kerb. I came to in hospital as doctors and nurses were doing tapestry work on my scalp. They gave me very hot tea and three biscuits and told me they were keeping me in over the weekend.

It was a bank holiday weekend and a great quietness reigned. There were no admissions or discharges or newspapers to interfere, and I was separated from the world by thick plate glass windows which streamed with rivulets of rain. Inside, all was peace. The other chaps supplied me with barley water, toothpaste, kitchen paper and samosas, as I've said. It was one of the most healing weekends I have ever had.

I learned that waiting was an integral part of hospital life, and it should be provided for

If all this sounds too good to be true, it's what happened. But I'm aware of other sides too, because an organisation as big as the NHS is also patchy. I've visited hospital wards, convalescent homes, and homes without number over the years as part of my job. Now I realise my status could change from a visitor to an inmate and that is a different matter.

The standard of equipment has certainly gone up for oldies, which is marvellous, and the nurses and carers are generally considerate and kind – sometimes far beyond the command of duty and certainly beyond what they're paid – but the advance in electronics isn't always matched by the provision of cuddles and genuine interest in the minds of aged people and the way they work. Sedation may be convenient but it

'It's alright for you. You won't have to go through the grieving process'

is not the standard answer to the distress the aged can experience. Also, old people are vulnerable because they need someone to fight their corner, someone who is not afraid to ask questions or be put off by shallow, pass-the-buck answers. There is a real shortage of dedicated cleaners. Come back matrons – all is forgiven!

To return to the happier side, I was touched by the aftercare of the NHS. Among a selection of examples I could quote are the following: a lady, probably a social worker, came to see me in hospital to make sure there was someone who would see to me back home, who would do my shopping and make me a cuppa; full marks also to the tea lady who danced around her trolley to entertain us after we woke up bleary-eyed. Also, praise is due to the constant stream of visitors, with or without trolleys, providing us with newspapers, aftershave, menu choices and assorted religious support.

I learnt very important spiritual lessons in hospital. In the waiting room for cancer treatments one young man was awfully worried that his hair would fall out, although he had been assured it would grow back after his 'chemo' was over. A girl from the other side of the waiting room got up and bent over him. I couldn't catch her exact words

but she seemed to be telling him something like this: 'Don't worry if your girlfriend stands you up because your hair falls out, I'd love to go out with you, and what's more, we'll go dutch.'

In seminaries they tell you a lot about original sin but in hospital you get lessons in original virtue. I remembered what one of my teachers had said to me: 'Hell is where people hate you. Heaven is where they help you.' It's that simple. Hospitals for me have been the latter. I've been lucky.

'Mum, hi... It's bad news, he's got the all-clear'

The highest mystery

JOHN MICHELL

wonders at this year's crop circles. Photographs by **LUCY PRINGLE**

The superb crop of circles, of which these examples were a part, centred upon Avebury and were mostly, as usual, in Wiltshire, spilling over into Hants, Oxon and Sussex.

The like of these magnificent formations had never before been seen – more beautiful and enigmatic than ever. Many of the designs were geometrical, expressing certain number combinations and continuing a process of esoteric instruction that has been evident for some years.

This is the finest art and the highest mystery of our age. Some people are frightened by the crop circle phenomenon because of its implications. The press are overawed by it and never mention it, except jokily. That is why we report on it each year. Oldie readers are mature enough to be told what is going on, making sense of it if they can, or simply enjoying the pictures.

This is the finest art and the highest mystery of our age

Top: Waylands Smithy, Oxfordshire
Above: East Field, Alton Priors, Wiltshire
Right: Woolstone Hill, Uffington, Oxon

Top: Avebury Avenue, Wiltshire
Above: Aldbourne, Wiltshire

*'I like these restaurants where you can
see the chef at work'*

The world according to
Enfield Snr

The dreadful spectacle of sport

AS I WRITE, the Ashes are all before us, and whether I watch them or not depends on how we are getting on at the time. My only interest in sport lies in watching Englishmen beating up foreigners, and if that is happening, I can watch almost anything, bar swimming which is unbearably dull.

When it comes to the Ashes, it is usually them beating us up, and this is such a dreadful spectacle that I have to switch the box off. If there are moments, though, when we seem to be holding our own, I shall be glued to it for as long as it lasts.

This being my view of sport, I have not taken much interest in Wimbledon since the days of Virginia Wade. Watching two foreigners playing pat-ball seems to me a silly way to spend one's time, though it is very popular with women. As Tim Henman got his *Nunc Dimittis* rather earlier than usual this year, I thought that I could give the rest of it a miss, but then I heard that there was a young Scotchman called Murray who was doing well, so I watched him and he won the first two sets.

I was much impressed by the generosity of the watchers. Although he was, after all, a Scotchman, and the crowd predominantly English, they and I adopted him as one of us, and there we sat, they at Wimbledon and I at home, all of us willing him to win. Now this was a great contrast to the football World Cup. As you may remember, when the Scots were knocked out of the World Cup but we English were still in, instead of rallying behind their fellow islanders, they kept hoping we would lose, and cheering for whoever was against us. They did this quite openly and I thought it was mean-spirited of them at the time, and doubly so when you consider the matter of the Ladies World Curling Championship.

Curling is a sport about which most of us know little. It seems to be a sort of bowls played on ice in countries with cold winters, such as Scotland and Canada. In 2002 the Ladies World Final was between Scotland and Switzerland, and they put it on our television countrywide. I think the whole of England watched, desperate for these nice Scotch ladies to win. When they did, we

leapt in the air, punched the sofa cushions and shouted 'Yes!' although we understood almost nothing of what was going on.

The winning shot was played by Rhona Martin, the Scotch captain, and to show you how mysterious the game is, I will quote part of her description of the shot itself: 'I was happy as I approached it as the house was open. I always ask the girls to clear me four feet to drive through. It was slightly tricky but it was a routine draw. I could come off it or draw to the left of it. I was quite happy with the line of it and the way it was going. Then it was up to the sweepers. After it left my hand it was their judgement call on whether it should be swept for weight. I didn't see it go into the house because the sweepers had moved behind it. It was only when Janice leaped in the air that I thought "Oh, we've won!"' I cannot think of another piece of prose which appeals so vividly to the imagination while conveying almost nothing to the understanding, for which reason I have kept it carefully for all this time.

My only interest in sport lies in watching Englishmen beating up foreigners

Now, bearing in mind our generous support of the Scotch Ladies Curling Team and the shabby hostility of the Scotch to the England Men's Football Team, I thought it was very decent of us to be cheering for this Murray. He was playing an Argentinian who conducted himself in a quiet and gentlemanly manner, which is uncommon in a game which seems to be given over to men who behave like hooligans and women who grunt like animals. Murray was all right when winning, but when things went against him he became a hooligan, ranting and swearing at the umpire in the usual way, so I went off him. 'Well,' I thought, 'he is just another foreigner, and you are watching two foreigners playing pat-ball, which is a silly way to spend the time,' so I stopped. If that Murray is back next year, if I watch him at all, I shall restrain my generous impulses and cheer for the other fellow, to redress the balance in the matter of the Ladies World Curling Championship and the England Football Team.

Who could ask for anything more?

*Betsy Blair married Gene Kelly when she was just 17, but that was just the start of her adventures in Hollywood. She talks to **ALICE PITMAN** about her life and loves*

The actress, Betsy Blair, has forgotten about our interview. She answers the door of her beautiful north London home and gives a self-deprecating chortle of apology. I suggest coming back later, but Betsy will not hear of it. With take-me-as-you-find-me breeziness, she invites me in to share her breakfast (tinned prunes and apricots). We sit in her kitchen diner. The room has a friendly, unflashy feel; house plants, books and a large Welsh dresser peppered with family ephemera, including photographs of her second husband, the late film director Karel Reisz. The walls abound with framed pictures from their grandchildren and modern art.

Betsy looks much younger than her 81 years, with an open face and attractive gravelly voice that oozes a serene self-assurance aeons away from the timid tones of the shy schoolmistress, Clara, in the 1955 cinematic classic, *Marty*, the role for which she is most remembered.

Still discernible, however, is the warm ebullience that must have been evident in the 16-year-old chorus girl who first caught the eye of up-and-coming dancer, Gene Kelly, when she turned up a day early for an audition in 1940.

'I thought he was the busboy because he was moving tables and chairs around,' recalls Betsy, smiling. 'He told me I'd come on the wrong day and I told him he was wrong. As I was leaving he called after me, "Are you a dancer?" I said, "Yes". Then he called, "Are you a good dancer?"

I said, "Very", in a rather snooty way. The next day when I arrived along with 600 or so other girls, it turned out he was the choreographer – he grinned at me and I was terribly embarrassed!'

They fell in love and married when Betsy was 17. Gene Kelly was her Svengali. 'He gave me my education. I didn't know anything really. I didn't know classical music, or anything about politics. He took me everywhere and showed me everything.'

They arrived in Hollywood on Pearl Harbor Day in 1941. Gene Kelly was cast opposite Judy Garland in *Me and My Girl* and from that moment his rise was meteoric – highlights being such legendary films as *An American in Paris*

and *Singing in the Rain*. They had a daughter, Kerry, now a psychoanalyst, and became known for their Saturday night parties where the guest list might include Noël Coward, Greta Garbo, Cary Grant and George Cukor. Marilyn Monroe also came to the house. 'She was sensational. I could see that she might easily be irresistible to men – you could sort of picture her in bed, I guess.'

Wasn't all this Hollywood glitz overwhelming for an unworldly adolescent from New Jersey?

'Not at all! The fact that they were stars didn't matter to me. It seemed normal, as I didn't know any different! I was happy with whatever happened.'

Betsy's own acting career, which was just beginning to take off, was abruptly curtailed by the McCarthy witch-hunts. In 1950 Betsy – who made no secret of her Marxist activism – was denounced as belonging to 'a nest of Reds'. The film offers soon dried up.

She had been blacklisted for four years when the script arrived for *Marty*. She loved it at once and auditioned for the part of Clara three times. 'As I was leaving the third audition the secretary whispered to me, "I think you've got the part... The Great Stone Face, Burt Lancaster, one of the three producers, had a tear in his eye."'

The part was indeed hers, but only if she wrote a letter to Congress that would clear her name politically. 'This meant I had to go and rat on my friends, name names, say I was sorry I was ever left-wing, that I was mistaken, that I loved America. I tried to write it, but all I could say was that I loved America, that we had a great constitution and that I would never do anything against it... but that wasn't what they wanted.'

It was Gene Kelly, wielding his star power, that ensured Betsy eventually secured the part.

'Gene went raging into Dore Shary's office – he was the Head of MGM – and said, "Listen Dore, you know Betsy, you play charades with her on

Gene gave me my education... I didn't know classical music, or anything about politics. He took me everywhere and showed me everything

Saturday night, you know she's not going to overthrow the government! Do something about this, or I'll stop shooting". For Gene to pull out in the middle of a film would have been a disaster! So MGM vouched for me to the American Legion in Washington which meant that I could be in *Marty*.'

The conversation returns inexorably to Gene Kelly. I ask Betsy whether he had a favourite dancing partner.

'Well he certainly loved dancing with Judy [Garland]. She was so generous and

Betsy in *Marty* with Earnest Borgnine in 1955

helpful and so much fun. People talk about the tragedy of her life, but I agree with Mickey Rooney who always said, "Judy tragic? What're you talking about? She was a great girl!"'

Was there any friendly rivalry between Gene Kelly and Fred Astaire?

'Gene admired Fred Astaire enormously, but Gene was a different kind of dancer. He had a whole other vision of the world. Fred Astaire was more into society – he would have liked to have been English! The Astaires moved with the oil crowd, the racetrack and all that. We were not like that at all. We were New York street kids. Gene was a working-class boy and he was going to bring dance to people who didn't go to the opera, or the ballet. He was going to make everyone feel that they could stomp about in the rain, or dance down the street. As soon as we got to Hollywood, Gene realised it was the place for him, he knew that he could reach the world better through the movies.'

Her marriage to Gene Kelly lasted 16 years. Betsy acknowledges that it was she who ended the marriage, although they remained good friends until his death in 1996. There was a tendency on Kelly's part to infantilise her and this proved ultimately unfulfilling. 'I was his little angel, his beloved playmate, he wanted to have and keep forever the girl I was, shaped by his care and love.'

By the late 1950s she had left Kelly, moved to Paris and fallen in love with the French actor,

Roger Pigaut. Her new friends included Simone Signoret, Yves Montand and Marguerite Duras. During this period she acted in several critically acclaimed European films, including Antonioni's *Il Grido* (The Cry) and *Calle Mayor*.

So where did she get such a talent for languages?

'Oh, I don't have a talent! I was dubbed! I spoke French, so I spoke French in some scenes – but when it was a difficult scene emotionally, I spoke English. Nobody minded and it was fun, I was having a good time, feeling a bit full of myself, as if I had a great gift for languages.'

In 1962 Betsy married the film-maker, Karel Reisz (*Saturday Night and Sunday Morning, This Sporting Life*). They moved to London where they lived happily – in this same house – for forty years until his death in 2002. Betsy recently wrote her memoirs, *The Memory of All That*, which ends at the point of her second marriage.

'Karel wasn't a man for publicity,' explains Betsy. She talks of his modesty, his desire for privacy without being reclusive. She remembers showing him a passage from her manuscript describing his amazing blue eyes and the fact that he had better teeth than any Englishman. 'Don't say amazing,' Karel told her, 'you should take that out.'

Betsy is toying with the idea of writing about her life with Karel. She loves writing, and wishes she had known years ago how enjoyable it was going to be.

'Karel was a very special man,' she says wistfully. 'I miss everything about him. Everything. Nobody touches you when you're old. I mean your grandchildren hug you, friends kiss you, but it's not the same. It's not sex: it's the intimacy. And of course I miss the humour and the fun... It's funny, but when my book came out, friends read it and said, "Well I have to tell you, Betsy, I'm in love with Gene". And strangers at book signings came up to me and said, "I don't know how you could have left him!" Sometimes, if I see Gene in an old movie, I think, "Yeah, he was really something, how could I have left him?!"'

'I've been very lucky,' Betsy concludes, 'I've been married to two exceptional men. My memories are of warmth and laughter and the joy of a creative life.'

As her first husband once sang in *I Got Rhythm* – Betsy's favourite Gene Kelly number – who could ask for anything more?

There's a cat in my soup

GEORGE PERKIN *was invited to a nearby primary school to tell the children about the local changes he had seen – but they only had ears for his more gory stories...*

Our local primary school, was inviting residents who had lived long in the area to talk to children about the changes they had seen. It seemed an original idea. And I had, after all, lived 40 years in this London terrace house.

But the sort of obvious socio-economic changes that I had witnessed – the fact that my house, built circa 1870 for the railway workers for £90, would now sell for £450,000 – would not fire the imaginations of young children.

So a teacher from the school came round to discuss the matter. What age, I asked, would the children be? Between the ages of seven and eleven. What changes, he asked, would I like to talk about? Well, I suggested, there were nine children in this two-bedroom house when I came, and now most houses were occupied by one or two people. 'That's fine,' he said. And then, I offered, many of these houses still had outside toilets. 'They'd love that,' he said. Encouraged, I mentioned Mrs Radwell next door who was 94 and had refused to have electricity and who died pulling a heavy old mangle onto herself. 'Perfect,' he said, and a date was fixed.

Came the day, and I arrived with anecdotes, a few photos, and a certain amount of nervous tension. I was greeted in the staff common-room by Emily and Alice – two immaculate tiny tots who were to escort me to the classroom, which they did with immaculate manners. In the classroom, the young lady in charge awaited my arrival. 'I'll just take them for a run to quieten them down before we start.'

A clatter of footsteps heralded the children's return, and I was surrounded by thirty pairs of eyes looking up at me from the floor. There was no going back, and I plunged boldly into my prepared anecdotes: the nine children in my house, the outside toilets, Mrs Radwell's electricity and mangle and other points of interest. I also handed round a photo of a girl outside my house in a long Laura Ashley gown pushing a pram.

'What did you wear?' one little girl suddenly asked. 'Well,' I offered rather lamely, 'I would not have gone out at weekends without my tweed sports coat, corduroy trousers and, of course, a brightly coloured tie.' This provoked laughter. What about T-shirts? Nobody, I said, had heard of T-shirts.

'What did you eat?' a little boy shyly ventured. Again, I wished I could have

Pandemonium broke out instantly. Screams of excited laughter. How long had the cat been there? Was it very dead?

said wild boar and capons roasted on spits. 'Actually,' I said, 'I had never been into a supermarket,' which was true – they had barely arrived – and most of my shopping was done in the Hal and Beef Stores opposite. Did I have a microwave? No microwave. Prompting me also to recall that 40 years ago I was still holding out against television. 'But what did you do instead?' one little boy asked in disbelief. What a good question.

In the midst of all this, one tiny girl suddenly drifted off into a private reverie. 'We moved into our house with my sister

and Mummy, and afterwards she had a baby and then Daddy arrived.' This piece of information was considered in silence, rescued by a little boy with a roguish grin. 'Were you in the war?'

I hadn't come to talk about the war. So I answered briefly, hoping to put him off. Yes, I was in the navy. What, a sailor? Yes, a sailor. On a warship? Yes. What sort of food did I eat on the warship? Actually, it was very bad – not quite maggots and scurvy, but the next thing.

As there seemed no escape, I told how there was a big kitchen called a galley, and in it was a huge cauldron always bubbling with soup, and we used to go with our mugs and fill them up. And then, before I could think whether it was suitable or not, I had launched into a story widely circulated on the ship: one day the soup boiled low in the cauldron, and at the bottom they found the ship's cat...

Pandemonium broke out instantly. Screams of excited laughter. How long had it been there? Was it very dead? What did the soup taste like? On and on. At this point, the young lady in charge thought it time to step in, terminate the proceedings, and thank our visitor for coming.

Two weeks later, a thick envelope fell onto the doormat, and in it were 30 letters from the children, done in their best handwriting, some dramatically illustrated. 'I rilly injod it,' wrote James. 'It was funy wen you told us about the soop.' There were several more on these lines. Daisy, obviously more advanced, said she had found the cat at the bottom of the soup 'particularly interesting' and illustrated her letter with an epic scene. In fact, the cat in the soup was a smash hit with most. In close competition, Francesca loved it 'when the mangl fell on your naber,' Top marks to the school for an imaginative venture. And so, trying not to think how these charming, well-mannered, spontaneous children might be in ten years time, I gathered up the letters and put them in an album.

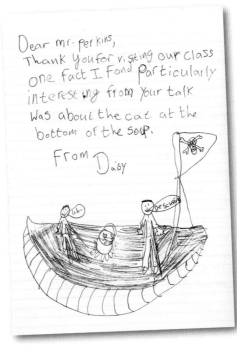

Left: The children wrote to George Perkin to thank him for his talk

SUBSCRIBE TO THE OLDIE

A message from the editor...

Richard Ingrams

'Although *The Oldie* has been going for fifteen years, it is still my impression that there are masses of people who have never heard of it, let alone seen a copy. This in turn persuades me that we have yet to achieve our full potential as a force for good in the world.

If you are one of the unblessed, I hope that this brief overview fires your enthusiasm for the quality, diversity and idiosyncrasy of the magazine's contents and contributors.

I look forward to welcoming you to our loyal and ever-growing readership.'

Save up to £57

How would you like a monthly magazine which is...

- **unpredictable** and **eclectic**, and
- where Britain's best writers express themselves freely and passionately
- where **books and the arts** are reviewed without mercy
- with **no whiff of a political agenda** and
- a **sanctuary** for all who are irritated by our celebrity-obsessed media and culture
- full of **cartoons** and is **very funny**

A Magazine that dares to be interesting, and celebrates the unusual and eccentric

It's wry, it's funny, it's eccentric – I read it with delight
Terry Wogan

THE VERY BEST COLUMNISTS

Miles Kington • Edward Enfield • Dr Thomas Stuttaford

• John Sweeney • Mavis Nicholson • Virginia Ironside • Rosie Boycott

'If you're happy and you know it clap your hands'

CHRISTMAS SOLVED!

Make it a gift sub for you or your friends:
one for £32.50 (save £6.50 off the shop price)
two for £60 (save £18)
three for £81 (save £36)
four for £99! (save £57)

Complete the form below (photocopy the page if you prefer) and send to:

The Oldie Magazine, FREEPOST RRAJ-AGER-LEAK, 800 Guillat Avenue, Kent Science Park, Sittingbourne ME9 8GU (no stamp required within the UK)

OR CALL 01795 592 893 QUOTING **AN2007**

This offer closes 30th April, 2008

☐ **YES,** I want to subscribe myself and the additional names below to The Oldie for the total of £ _____

| Purchaser's Name |
| Address |
| |
| |
| Postcode _____ Email _____ |

I would like to pay by either:

☐ Cheque enclosed (payable to Oldie Publications Ltd)
or:

☐ Please charge my credit/debit card:

☐ Visa ☐ Mastercard ☐ Switch/Maestro (Issue No ☐☐)
Card Number

☐☐☐☐ ☐☐☐☐ ☐☐☐☐ ☐☐☐☐

Start date ☐☐☐☐ Expiry date ☐☐☐☐
Signature

☐☐☐☐☐☐ Date ☐☐☐☐

RECIPIENTS' DETAILS

| Name |
| Address |
| |
| Postcode _____ Email _____ |
| Name |
| Address |
| |
| Postcode _____ Email _____ |
| Name |
| Address |
| |
| Postcode _____ Email _____ |
| Name |
| Address |
| |
| Postcode _____ Email _____ |

From time to time The Oldie may contact you with details of its products and services. Please tick here if you object to receiving such information by post ☐

We occasionally pass your details onto carefully selected companies whose products and services we feel may be of interest to you. Please tick here if you object to receiving such information by post ☐

AXEL SCHEFFLER

Gotta lotta bottle

Can a milkman's life really be full of spies, sexual intrigue and skulduggery?
Well, yes, actually, it can, reveals recently retired milkie, **PHIL WARK**

I know what you are thinking. Is it true what they say about milkmen? All those housewives? Well, it's not a myth, though I think that it's rare. But when a lady in her forties regularly pays you stark naked, you have to wonder. Is she a naturist? Has she got early Alzheimer's, or is she looking for a bit of fun? With a young, nubile partner at home, I wasn't really interested.

Then there was a pleasant Dutch lady whose sexual frustration was manifest, although her approach was somewhat surreal. 'My husband is away. I drove him to the airport today. He's in Japan. And look what I found on the floor after he had gone.'

She places a two-inch screw on the table next to my cup of tea.

'It's a nice screw, isn't it?' she says.

'It's… very nice.' I sip my tea.

'Would you like this nice screw?'

'Actually, I've got lots of screws at home.'

I began my career on London's milk rounds in 1982. Friends told me it was a dying business. They were right, but it was a slow death, and I've only just given up the ghost. In those days if you drove north from central London there was a milk depot in every metropolitan village. Supermarket giants like Sainsbury's sold milk, but at the same price as your milkman. Virtually every household had their milk delivered.

Today all but one of those depots have closed down and there are none in central London – the temptation for the main players to cash in on prime property locations having been too great to resist. The big companies have also abandoned retail deliveries, leaving them to franchisees, few of whom have survived.

And so, after a week at Milkman University, being schooled and examined in milkman paperwork and customer relations, I turned up at West Hampstead depot to begin my hands-on training. After a week with a roundsman, I was given a round in Hampstead.

'Mr Foot. Call daily,' read the roundsbook. 'Would you like some tea?' asked the Leader of the Opposition.

'Yes, please.' I was left of Militant at the time and he was an old-time socialist, and we had fine talk and numerous arguments. It was close to election time and I inevitably asked him about Labour's chances of defeating the Iron Lady. He predicted a Labour win with a majority of fifty to sixty seats.

The coda to this story is that I was once approached by a well-known Hampstead vagrant after a cup of tea with Mr Foot.

'Been to see Michael?' he asked.

'Yes,' I answered. 'He thinks Labour can win.'

'He ain't got a bleedin' clue,' said the prescient vagrant.

The judgment was harsh but Foot did lose heavily in the 1983 election. The tramp was rather better dressed than Michael.

'It's a nice screw, isn't it?' she says. 'It's very nice.' I sip my tea. 'Would you like this nice screw?' she asks. 'Actually, I've got lots of screws at home…'

Subsequently I worked on a round in NW1 where I served a legendary actor who, I believe, is still just about alive, so I can't really offer a name. One day, on receiving his pint of gold top, he made an unusual request. It seemed that he wanted to see my 'willy'. Just see it, no touching. I answered that there wasn't a lot to see but he was insistent, telling me that Bob, his regular milkman, always showed him his 'willy'. I obliged. He gave me a £10 tip. All part of the service, though I hadn't been briefed about such occasions at Milkman University.

The Serious Crimes Squad raided the depot at West Hampstead: six milkmen were arrested, lockers and cars searched. There had been a post-train robbery at Euston. Apart from cash and cards, many thousands of milk tokens had been purloined. These traceable tokens began to be presented by roundsmen at West Hampstead. Milkmen working in affluent areas like Golders Green, where tokens were rarely offered in payment, suddenly began presenting 80 or 90 a week, each worth about £2.50.

Then there was the Sunday overtime: well paid, about thirty calls, mainly shops, and one perk, the London Zoo Trojan Horse job. Although I never indulged in this scam, others did. The drops on Sunday were done in a truck, the back of which was covered. It was the last call and the vehicle was almost empty. At the Zoo, you pressed a bell at the tradesman's entrance and spoke into an intercom. The staff in the restaurant let you in. You drove in and dropped about 100 pints of milk off. Nice people, cup of tea, 'Cheerio, see you next week.' Outside you could reverse the truck about twenty yards, which left you next to an alley which led into the Zoo. A quick look around; open up the back. 'Quickly kids!' Out they would stream – fifteen to twenty kids, four or five mothers, grannies, aunties, neighbours.

MI5 was a strange drop. Naturally there was heavy security. 'Please state the nature of your business.' 'It's the milkman.' Long pause. 'Your entrance is confirmed.'

Once through the remotely controlled doors, you drove down a ramp and parked in a slot with underground illumination. Security emerged with what looked a little like a lawn strimmer and poked about underneath the vehicle looking for bombs. It took about five minutes to be cleared. These security men never looked in the back of the vehicle. I could have had bin Laden and thirty Taliban with grenades and Kalashnikovs in the back.

Nothing lasts forever. The supermarkets introduced the cheap four-pint poly-bottle, sales dropped as the working and lower middle classes started to buy milk with the weekly shop; rounds were broken up, depots closed down. History marches on.

Encounter with a killer

*The unpleasant man with sickly yellow skin had followed **S D LUKAC** before.
But this time she was trapped on the Underground – how would she escape?*

I was a fully-fledged career girl before I told anyone about my encounter with John Reginald Halliday Christie. That is how I remember him described on *BBC News* at the time.

We were then living in Shepherd's Bush, and every time I came home for the school holidays the man would be there, stalking me, usually from the opposite side of the street, whenever I ran errands for my mother or went for walks with the son of friends who lived nearby.

S D Lukac, aged 17, in 1953

He seemed extremely tall, probably because he was rake-thin. His yellow, sickly-looking skin was stretched taut on his skull, which had greasy bits of hair stuck to it here and there. He wore wire-rimmed glasses and a filthy mac, whatever the season. He had a very peculiar smell about him.

It never occurred to me either to tell my parents or to go to the police. Having experienced war in Poland and other countries, I took a lot in my stride. Only once did I want to run to a nearby policeman: that was when the man cornered me among the glass showcases of Lilley and Skinner's. But I was too shy and thought that they would treat me simply as a panicky schoolgirl.

One day, towards the end of the Christmas holidays, I had to collect something from a jeweller's in Edgware Road. It was a horrible day: sleet, snow, wind, slippery pavements, and the sort of weather into which a good master wouldn't wish to let his dog out.

On my way to the Hammersmith and City line, the man caught up with me. He came abreast saying 'Don't do what I did', and opened his dirty mac to demonstrate clear signs that he had slipped and fallen into the filthy brew on the pavement.

He followed me to the ticket office, placing himself behind me. I bought my ticket without thinking that he would now know how far I would be travelling.

As I entered the empty carriage, he followed and sat in the seat which was at ninety degrees to mine

It was the 'dead' hour, around eleven in the morning, and as I entered the empty carriage he followed and sat in the seat at ninety degrees to mine, from where he observed me closely.

I sat next to the glass partition and, from behind the magazine I was pretending to read, I watched him uneasily.

Suddenly, he moved next to me. He put his arm around me, above my shoulders, the circle of his arms completed by an open newspaper. 'Have you seen this article?' he said. 'No.' I pushed him away. The train was slowly approaching Ladbroke Grove. I was terrified. I thought: if I leave the moment the doors open, he will rush out and grab me in the deserted

Notorious killer John Christie in the early fifties

station. I waited. He seemed uncertain of his next move. I held out until I heard the 'sigh' signalling that the pneumatic doors were about to close, and rushed out, my knees buckling under me. He tried to follow, but was too slow.

After a while, I continued my journey to Edgware Road and returned home.

I didn't say anything to my parents then, nor for many years. My mother did remark that I looked pretty awful when I came back, but I ignored it.

It was time to prepare for the next term. I was ironing my clothes when I heard the BBC announce on the news that police were seeking to question one John Reginald Halliday Christie of 10 Rillington Place, Notting Hill. I made no connection: at the time, my family only read the Polish papers and those carried the latest news but very few, if any, photographs.

The last I heard before going back to school was that Christie had been apprehended by the police on Putney Bridge. Again, I made no connection.

It was only back at school that I finally found out just whom I had escaped from.

The nuns in our convent subscribed to the *Times*, but one girl in my form had special dispensation to receive the *Daily Telegraph*. Sitting in the library conservatory one day, stuck in my Livy, I looked up and saw the face of my stalker staring at me from behind my pal's shoulder.

I didn't think of him again until many years later, and that's when I first told my story.

Let my people stay!

AUSTIN MITCHELL

thinks the experience of older MPs is an undervalued asset in Parliament today – but not everyone agrees

Illustrations by
BOB GEARY

Age may not weary me, but the years condemn me to being one of a threatened species: old MPs. We work next door to a well-appointed, centrally-heated retirement home, the Lords, but in the Commons oldies who want to carry on doing a full-time job are seat-blockers, keeping the ambitious, thrusting young from what should rightfully be theirs.

There are three ages of politics. We come in, as Tony did, professing eternal devotion to our constituency and a passionate desire to serve it, while regarding it as a stepping stone to power. The aspirant age is devoted to mastering the MP's job and pushing for promotion. Some never get it or don't want to, but for most it leads to the second age of power, a prime time for Ministers, major, minor and Shadow. Last comes the third age, over the hill, ambition spent, skills perfected, and only one job to do. Some have climbed the lower slopes of power and returned, occasionally hurt. Some have fallen off; others never bothered or have never been chosen, for reasons so painful they'll only explain them in confidence and at length.

This should be a golden age of maturity. The oldies are out of the Great Game of Power. No one over fifty has any prospect of office, although like John Prescott (68) they can hang on in there. Oldies are experienced, battle-hardened, well qualified to make a major full-time contribution to Parliament and to constituencies, but they're under threat – and the older they are, the greater the threat. Like a threatened stand of trees, our dwindling band of oldies fears that the felling of one endangers all. Mates (72) has crashed, *felo*, or is it felled, *de se*. Lumberjacks have moved in on Cormack (67), and Dunwoody (76) may be under friendly chopping, but Tapsell (77) still towers, and Kaufman (76) looks safe. The lumber Jacks

and Jills are Party Apparatchaps who become more powerful as the election approaches. They'd love to clear the whole stand and replant with saplings. So we quake, exposed and impotent, to protect ourselves against a fashionable clamour for youth, vigour and all the foolish things we long since put away.

This fetish of youth hits this old and ageing country harder than most. The average age of MPs, 51 at the election, is lower than pre-war because more arrive in their twenties or thirties and more leave earlier. By contrast, China is ruled by a gerontocracy, while in the US age brings seniority and power; at 62 the average age of the new Congress is the oldest in US history. In Britain, however, youthful looks and vacuity are preferred. Age is acceptable only in local government: sixty per cent of councillors are over sixty because so few want to do the job. Parties want to make themselves more representative in terms of ethnicity and gender, but not age, despite an ageing electorate. They'd prefer to drive out older MPs to appeal to what Tony Blair mistakenly described as a 'young country', and to young electors who don't vote anyway.

The consequences can be dramatic, as in the defenestration of Sir Patrick Cormack, and as re-selection gets under way there will be others. Yet the pressure is mainly silent and unpublicised as some MPs pack up quietly and go. Tony Benn advised me, 'Never say you're going. Once you do you're a dead duck.' So we proclaim our desire to stay on – and most mean it, although a few are awaiting an offer of a peerage.

The MP's job has become steadily more pressured in my thirty years. Our mail increases exponentially, and the select committees and 440 All Party Groups produce a lot of work. Local parties are no longer providing the support of agents and councillors, so MPs and their allowances keep local parties going. We're on a treadmill going faster every year. We have staffs to cope,

AGEISM
IN THE COMMONS
CONCERN

but that means we're also running a small business cum internet café, as we struggle to blog, offer websites and cope with floods of email. Yet we oldies have adjusted well to heightened activity, reduced power, and a world where endless minutiae replace major influence. We've coped because, unlike the young and thrusting First Agers who are after power and a ministerial job, we find being an MP satisfying in itself. And apart from Ken Clarke, we've nothing much else to do.

Third Agers dance to a different tune because they're no longer contenders. Ambition is spent, achieved and lost, or never fulfilled. This makes them less manageable by whips who dangle hopes of promotion before the young but have little to offer the old, not even early nights these days. Parties have little desire to prolong the

Most oldie MPs struggle on, and it's they who keep the Commons alive. Every tribe needs its elders

active parliamentary life of troublesome oldies who are better replaced by malleable youngsters who'll talk the talk and submit to any humiliation for promotion. Oldies mean trouble.

Older MPs fade away, not disappearing from the parliamentary scene that no one outside is interested in, but from the media whose producers and journalists are dedicated followers of fashion and prefer the young and the rising to the old and verbose. We're written out of cast lists and contact books and no longer invited on *Any Questions*, television or even local media, and watch the whipper-snappers taunting Menzies Campbell (66) about being too old to be leader of anything but Age Concern.

We measure out our lives in the receding of Tony Blair's hairline, but in Parliament age creeps up unnoticed. The place looks more like a youth club with hundreds of researchers,

staffs, lobbyists and cause-pushers thronging Portcullis House. History began in 1997 and anything before that is archaeology. My standard response when asked how to spell my name – 'Austin, like the car' – now produces blank looks.

The tipping point came, suddenly, last year. A back problem had me (72) staggering round on walking sticks. Disability and misfortune are always noticed in the Commons. In death there is hope. So suddenly people began to ask whether I'd be standing again and showing an interest in my seat. Bright young things asked about Grimsby. Some even visited or offered to speak to the Grimsby Labour Party. I had become, without realising it, a threatened species. Some oldies subside into dignified obsolescence as Deputy Speakers or Members of the Chairman's Panel. A lucky few become Select Committee chairs. Others keep their heads down, like the oldest of all, Piara Khabra (82, but possibly older). But most struggle on and it's they who keep the Commons alive.

Every tribe needs its elders and so do the Commons People. Where would we be without Gwyneth Dunwoody on transport, Paul Flynn (72) and Frank Field (64) on pensions, Glenda Jackson (70), and David Winnick (73) on Blair's Wars, Kaufman on Israel and the media, Kelvin Hopkins (65) on Europe, Peter Tapsell and Ken Clarke (66) on economic policy, Ian Paisley (80) on Northern Ireland, Dennis Skinner on everything?

Parties would be more malleable if they lost the old, for whom the past is another (often a better) party because they were selected by different parties pursuing different policies and purposes, many of which have since been chucked overboard. The Tories could be blandished into Blairism for Beginners were it not resisted by disciples of Mrs Thatcher, like Bill Cash (66) and Edward Leigh (56, but looking older) and the Wintertons (68 and 66). Labour would have been totally lobotomised without Old Labour MPs who remember another way of doing things, although it's been turned into a nightmare to frighten the young. Today's parties change colour to suit the moment and formulate policies for sales not sense. So the old are the only check on the voyage to vacuity, which makes them an even bigger nuisance.

There is a case for term limits on Ministers who do two jobs and peter out. There's a far stronger one for time limiting Prime Ministers, since all recent ones have been broken or barmy after eight years, although only Harold Wilson realised it. There's no such justification for purging old MPs or for getting rid of the experienced, the independent-minded, and anyone old enough not to be malleable. They are the backbone of the Commons. For their twenty or thirty years of membership has been a polishing process fitting them to make a bigger and better contribution than any other age group. They should be preserved. Let my people stay.

Far left: Austin Mitchell
Centre: Ken Clarke
Top: Gwyneth Dunwoody
Left: Tony Benn

It's totally bugging, innit?

We asked you guys to give us a heads up on the modern phrases that are, like, massively annoying to yourselves. **NICK PARKER** *rounds up the most irksome examples...*

Wicked!

Work-life balance

You're invading my personal space

Comfort zone

Wake-up call

24/7

HELP!

Railway rants

- There are delays on the Central line, the Circle line and the Hammersmith and City line. The Bakerloo line southbound is suspended. King's Cross station is closed due to a security alert. The Jubilee line is experiencing signalling problems in the Neasden area. There is a good service running on all other lines
(Which other lines are left?)

- Warning: professional pickpockets operate in this area

- Thank you for choosing to travel with South-Eastern Rail
(Except that South-Eastern Rail hold a monopoly over the route and therefore no choice was ever actually possible...)

- Your on-train team

- We would like to advise customers

- The next station stop will be Carlisle

- On behalf of myself

YOUR TOP 5 IRRITANTS

1. 'Have a nice day!'

2. 'Your call is important to us'

3. 'No probs!'

4. 'Chill out'

5. 'Bear with us'

station stop...

Telephone tirades

- Please hold the line. Your call is important to us
(Although not actually important enough for us to want to speak to you. So please keep holding...)

- Thank you for your patience
(I'm not being patient, I'm screaming – it's just that no-one can hear me, because I'm still on hold...)

- Your call may be monitored for security reasons
(What security reasons?)

- Your call may be monitored for staff training purposes
(Wait, I thought you were monitoring for security reasons?)

ILLUSTRATIONS BY STEVEN APPLEBY

Enjoy

Dude

I was gutted

Whatever

Talk to the hand

I was, like, totally...

Gobsmacked

Cheers, mate

There you go

I'm so not

Retail rages

- Clinically proven
(by our own marketing department)

- Anti-ageing

- Up for grabs!

- Because you're worth it

- Classic *(When used to describe things that are just normal, like calling Ready-salted a 'classic flavour'.)*

- Limited-edition flavours *(Only twelve million lemon-flavoured jaffa cakes made this week...)*

TOOT PARP

HONK

MUST FI ALL THE PAGES ...

Dumbing downers

- **Back-to-back**
  Is 'consecutively' too high falutin'?

- **The run-up to Christmas**
  Previously known as 'Advent'

- **Pre-booking**
  What other kind of booking is there?

- **Young girls**
  Tautological. Except when used to distinguish from simply 'girls'. Used these days to mean any woman under the age of forty, because saying 'woman' would just sound too old and uncool...

- **At this moment in time**
  What, 'now' you mean?

Chris Donald's rant

'I hate the word "gateway", which has become popular in marketing. Estate agents describing a "gateway opportunity" for example. That'll be a shop next to a road. And I particularly don't like it when an unremarkable town describes itself as a "gateway" to some local, or not so local, attraction. Wooler in Northumberland is marketed as "the gateway to the Cheviots". It should more properly be called "the arsehole of the Cheviots". I'm sure that would attract more tourists.

'And I don't like it when a business becomes a "one-stop shop". A blacksmiths used to be the place to go for horse hooves, buckets, plough repairs, all sorts of things. But smithies didn't feel the need to describe their shed as a "one-stop shop". They're only saying it because it rhymes, not because it means anything worth saying.

'And I don't like people who describe themselves as "facilitators". All that means is that they provide a facility, ie, they do something. Everyone with a bloody job does something. The twats. The fact that you do something is not relevant to what you actually do.'

words (WĒRDS) words. n.

Boast no more your mighty deeds!

I HAVE ALWAYS thought that braggadocio is a good word. It came to mind recently when I heard a local tennis player blowing blue wind, as they say hereabouts, about his former greatness. He felt that, given the opportunity, he would have given Laver, or Borg, or Federer a run for their money; he was a braggadocio personified.

The word was coined by Edmund Spenser. In his day young Englishmen used to take off for the continent in spring and, as part of this holiday, a long stay in Italy was a tradition. There they developed a taste for Italian clothes, for fine Italian wines, and for exotic Italian regional food. When they returned to England, their exaggerated Italian manners, tales of conquest of Italian girls, and swaggering behaviour in general made them targets of stay-at-home satirists who called them macaronis after the Italian dish favoured by the lower orders. Spenser's word for a swaggering fop, braggadocio – the name of the allegorical figure of a coward in the Faerie Queene – he coined from brag plus an Italianate ending. It is a curious construction. 'Bragadoccio' or 'Bragadocchio' would have been more persuasive Italianate forms.

This creation of Spenser's brags and boasts of his great courage in rescuing a fair lady from a fate worse than death. She falls in love with him, of course. Enter various outraged champions who show him up for what he is: a liar and a scoundrel; they relieve him of the things he has stolen and drive him away humiliated. John Kelly, an *Oldie* reader from Dublin, asked me about Spenser's word.

AT AN *OLDIE* lunch last year, somebody – I'm pretty sure, Barry Cryer – asked me about the word kid: a child, a youngster, and in America, a term of endearment. Since then I've had a few more enquiries about the word, most of them expressing disapproval of this 'American trivialisation'.

The funny thing is, kid in the senses I have mentioned was commonly used in the greatest days of English literature. The playwrights Philip Massinger, Thomas Middleton and William Rowley have this in their collaboratively written play, *The Old*

Law (1618): 'I am old, you say, yes, parlous old, kids, and you mark me well.' In 1698 D'Urfey wrote in *Collin's Walk*: 'At her back a kid that cry'd, Still as she pinch'd it, fast was ty'd.' He also wrote: 'Send your kid home to me, I will care on it.'

So, it is not an Americanism of recent vintage. The original meaning – fawn, kitten, young goat – was first attested in the 12th century in an Anglo-Norman legal tract. It was probably used in England before that under Danelaw, in the 9th or 10th centuries; we find the word *kith*, a young goat, in Old Norse. The word is of Germanic origin as evidenced by German *Kitz*, *Kitze* which are

I heard a local tennis player boasting about his former greatness. A 'braggadocio' personified

from the Old High German *chizzi*, *kizzin*. The Old Teutonic origin was probably kittin, from unattested kithnin. The word was in Middle English as kide. Oxford points out that the final 'e' in kide is not explicable from the Old Norse *kith*, but that the initial 'k' makes it still more difficult to the refer to the word as any Old English type. At any rate, Mr Cryer, here's lookin' at you, kid.

I AM SADDENED sometimes by words I find here in County Waterford, where Irish was until recently the vernacular. Indeed the last monoglot Irish speaker died near Dungarvan, where I live, in 1943. A word I heard recently is trisk. It is a seaweed growing on submerged rocks; I haven't yet found out what its botanical name is, because the only modern Irish dictionary that has recorded the word doesn't tell me. It is from the Irish trioscar, defined by the great Father Dinneen's dictionary as wrack or sea-oak, bladder-wrack. The word has survived by being assimilated into the English of this district. I am reminded of a little poem written by a friend, Aidan Mathews. He called it *The Death of Irish*:

'The tide gone out for good,
Thirty-one words for seaweed
Whiten on the foreshore.'

DIARMAID Ó MUIRITHE

I've been tangoed!

At the Funky Monkey **DAEMIENNE SHEEHAN** learned how to make the perfect V...

In a moment of madness, I invited my boss to a tango class with me. On a weekday evening we met up, her in a form-fitting plunging-neckline dress of widow black and me in brown walking shoes, ratty gardening skirt and a translucent gold-flecked cardigan. Our two-hour tango class was in a dingy room above the Funky Monkey pub in south London. With its cracked walls, dim light and red leather armchairs lined against the walls like dance-hall contestants, it seemed the perfect place to learn the dance some say was born in the bordellos of Buenos Aires.

Behind the minibar, that only sold one lager, our tango master waited all alone. Despite the lack of company he did not appear too concerned, finally wandering over to explain the history of the dance dedicated to women. A short, plump man in his late forties with oily grey hair swept over a balding pate, Andy sported a goatee and moustache that hinted of a bygone era when perfumed hair tonic was in every man's washbag. Profusely sweating, he popped down beside us, his tiny feet seeming to hover above floorboards thoughtfully sprinkled with talcum powder. Andy looked like a tango master, and when he danced everything made sense: the grey hair gradually falling over his brow, his sad, bulging beagle eyes filled with the melancholy of an unrequited lover, his tiptoeing feet and delicately surging tummy.

But my boss was not impressed – not initially anyway. It went awry when Andy told us that there were no steps to the tango. 'You see,' Andy said, 'the appealing thing about the tango is that you make it up as you go along.'

'No steps? There must be some steps.' My boss threw me a horrified glance. 'How can we learn if there are no steps?'

'It's instinctual,' Andy assured us. 'Women are meant to be better because they have a lower centre of gravity, which improves balance.'

'But what if a tall woman dances with a short man?' I asked. 'Wouldn't her centre of gravity be wobbled?'

'A moot point,' said Andy. 'Many people debate that one.'

'What about male partners? We're not going to have to be men, are we?' I fretted.

'Well,' said Andy, 'usually there are more men.' He looked around as if one might be hiding behind the minibar.

But no, only two more women had arrived, wearing skirts that swayed and swooshed and shoes with straps.

With the tango it appeared Man marched onward and Woman kept him at bay, the way you might with any monster

'When there aren't men,' Andy continued doggedly, 'the women have to be men. But that can be good too: you learn what men have to put up with. It's not easy, I can tell you. Look, when you think of tango, what comes to mind?'

'Scent of a Woman,' I said swiftly.

'Ah,' Andy livened up. 'As it happens, that is not a bad tango, not bad at all. I'll do a few moves, you'll see what I mean about improvisation.'

Andy did his magic as I nudged my boss. 'See?' I whispered. 'Moves, that means steps; he just wants to emphasise the mystique of the tango.' My boss looked relieved. 'That's a step,' she barked out as Andy slid past. 'You did that twice – what step is that?'

Andy nipped it in the bud. 'We'll return to that later,' he said. 'First let's limber up by walking around the room to feel the beat of the tango.' Everyone began walking in a circle, but my boss and I could not get the beat. My boss sighed heavily. 'I need steps.' Fortunately, two men had arrived.

With admirable faith, Andy threw us all in at the deep end. 'Basically,' he said, 'the tango is walking. You walk backwards and he walks towards you. The woman decides how far he will go. And the man has to work his way around her and make sure she doesn't bump into anything. Women shouldn't look at the men's feet because they should feel which foot they step forward with. If it's the left, your right goes back. Men shouldn't look into the women's eyes either.'

Andy demonstrated, his impassive face looking like Al Pacino. With the tango, it appeared Man marched onward as Woman kept him at bay the way you might with any monster – by clutching his shoulders, maintaining a distance and walking backwards. The woman also took long, straight strides with an uncowed posture, resulting in a pleasing upside-down V stance as both sexes leaned into each other.

As it was, I skittered nervously, slope-shouldered and teetering as my partner tried not to look like a thoroughly unpleasant rapist. Andy finally came over to put me right. 'I hadn't realised I looked that terrified,' I said. 'Remember you're in control,' Andy said. Then my boss waylaid him.

'I don't understand this arm business. Am I doing it right?' she said, pushing mightily against a bespectacled ginger-head who obliged her with a perfect V-half.

'You're allowed to bend your arms,' Andy said.

'I didn't know that,' my boss said reproachfully. 'I need to know that. So I can bend my arms – what else can I do?'

Daemienne (not in her gardening shoes) and tango master Andy strut their stuff

'Your posture needs straightening up. Just lean against a wall as if you're trying to hold it up to get the V shape.' Marching over to the wall, my boss began pushing against it like Samson.

Andy moved us on to turns and sideways walking, with one particularly attractive move, the 'cruzada', where one foot is crossed in front or behind the other. There was also the snappy 'giro', where the man executes a sharp, mercurial turn.

I still had no idea where the beat was but could see my boss dancing with great determination. My partner, a tall Scottish man in black wearing loafers, grimly tried teaching me to cross my ankles as he moved sideways. 'You're supposed to feel it,' he said. A little later he remarked, 'Did you cross your ankles because you wanted to or because you guessed?'

'I guessed.'

'I'm doing something wrong then. You're supposed to want to cross your ankles,' he worried. 'Do you want to cross them now?'

'Not yet,' I said, 'but I'm sure I will soon.'

By now the intermediates had arrived and were dancing too. These, clearly, were the milongueros, or tango fanatics. As I watched open-mouthed, a handsome young man in his twenties over six feet tall transported a five-foot-tall lady in her early sixties across the floor, locking ankles gracefully and holding her with one hand underneath the small of her back as she flung herself backwards. What was most striking was their expressions – his admiring and hers proud and happy.

The tango master observed me calmly. 'The tango takes time,' he said, 'but it's a wonderful dance for anyone at all.'

'I think we'll try you on something a trifle milder Mrs Pennyworthy'

OLDIE MASTERS

A guide to neglected artists
No 62: PROFESSOR GERALD MOIRA 1867-1959

Return From Shopping
Oil on card, 25 x 30 inches. Circa 1935. Price on request.

It may come as a surprise to those who often sit beneath the Wigmore Hall frieze, 'The Striving of Humanity after the Elusiveness of Music in its Great Abstraction', that this is by the same artist.

Gerald Moira – or Giraldo de Moura, as he began – very successfully rode the styles during the turbulent years 1890-1950. It was only the President of the Royal Academy Frederick Leighton's casting vote that robbed him of his year's Gold Medal but, undaunted, he had established a swagger portrait practice by the early '90s and carried out a series of arts and crafts decorative schemes which made him very well-known. These friezes, of which those decorating the Trocadero Restaurant in Shaftesbury Avenue (1896) were

the best known, were designed and coloured by him, having been modelled in plaster and gesso by the sculptor Frank Lynn Jenkins. Numerous commissions followed, especially after he was appointed Professor of Mural and Decorative Painting at the Royal College of Art (1900-1922) and Principal of Edinburgh College of Art (1924-1932). Lloyds Register, the Central Criminal Courts and City Hall, Bristol, were among many other public buildings – as well as P&O Liners – that acquired his look. As fashions changed, so did his *fin-de-siècle* manner, cleverly combining Burne-Jones and Sargent. He became less smooth and more painterly, and his figure compositions more lively and less suavely composed.

An Arcadian England

IAIN BAIN *celebrates Samuel Palmer – unsung hero of English art...*

Samuel Palmer's work, although much loved and admired, remains too little known to the world at large. Of a hundred people who know of the work of Turner and Constable, probably fewer than ten have come across that of Palmer. But even without background knowledge, his work is certainly accessible and, unlike many present-day ephemeral 'concepts', it brings lasting pleasure.

Born in 1805, the son of a London bookseller and preacher, and from an early age steeped in the classics, Palmer was 19 when he met John Linnell – older, successful as a painter and eventually to be his father-in-law. Linnell introduced him to the great visionary artist and poet, William Blake, who became his mentor.

Palmer had already seen Blake's remarkable small wood engravings, which had been created in 1821 and produced for Dr John Thornton's *Pastorals of Virgil*. Enraptured, Palmer wrote of them: 'They are visions of little dells, and nooks, and corners of Paradise, models of the exquisitest pitch of intense poetry.

'I thought of their light and shade, and looking upon them I found no word to describe it. Intense depth, solemnity, and vivid brilliancy only coldly and partially describes them. There is in all such a mystic and dreamy glimmer as penetrates and kindles the innermost soul, and gives complete and unreserved delight, unlike the gaudy daylight of this world...'

'There is such a mystic and dreamy glimmer as penetrates and kindles the innermost soul...'

A sketchbook of 1824, a survivor of his son's later burning of many others, provides a fascinating record of the young Palmer's development under this influence. Glimmering light and a sense of the spiritual were thus to pervade much of Palmer's work during the years that followed when he settled in the Kentish village of Shoreham with a group of like-minded friends. They called themselves 'The Ancients' and rejected the ways of the modern world.

The originality of Palmer's work of this period was at a far remove from the naturalism of his time. Its unconventional handling, coupled with a powerful visionary imagination, produced paintings that many claim to be his finest, unmatched by those of his middle years after he left Shoreham in 1835 to travel for four years in Wales and Italy. His *Moonlight, a Landscape with Sheep* (see top right) – one of a group that he called his 'blacks' – and the blazing richness of his *Magic Apple Tree* (see below) are a remarkable record of his response to what he regarded as the paradise of the Kentish countryside. Nearly all of modest size, they are infused with a compelling poetry and sense of mystery.

One of several essays in an exhibition catalogue has a useful account of Palmer's part in the Old Water Colour Society and the linking period between the deaths of de Wint, Copley Fielding, and Cox and the coming of the younger landscape painters with their Pre-Raphaelite connections. Even here Palmer was hardly of the mainstream and his colour provoked the conventional critics to puzzled but grudging admiration. Leaving Shoreham and the pastoral idyll was in part provoked by the rural unrest of the times, and in part by the need to support his family with more saleable conventional work. Yet, as the exhibition clearly showed, this was done without losing his poetic response to landscape.

My own delight in Palmer was fostered 40 years ago when the great etchings of his later life could be found for quite modest prices. He took up etching in 1850 and although he was only to produce 17 plates before he died in 1881 – four of which were finished by his younger son – they are one of the glories of this exacting medium. They also mark a return to the spirit of his Shoreham days.

His effects were achieved with an unconventional use of line and

Top left: The Rising Moon, c.1855-7. Copyright British Museum

Bottom left: Engraving by William Blake, taken from Thornton's Pastorals of Virgil

Top this page: Moonlight, a Landscape with Sheep, c.1831-2. Copyright Tate

Right: The Magic Apple Tree, c.1830. Copyright Fitzwilliam Museum

The originality of Palmer's work of this period was at a far remove from the naturalism of his time

relied a good deal on careful, far from straightforward printing. When I had the good fortune to take experimental impressions from the copperplate for his *Lonely Tower*, a single print could take up to 30 minutes of preparation. The process involved nursing the shadow areas by slight dragging up of ink from the recessed lines, yet allowing the sparkle of lights and stars their full brightness. *The Rising Moon* of 1855-7 (see above left) has many such touches, as seen in the gleaming lamps in the windows of the distant house and the light on the church tower.

Palmer's influence has been lasting and the revival of his reputation can to some extent be attributed to the rediscovery and reissue of his etchings around eighty years ago in 1926. It can be seen in the work of a number of 20th-century artists. One of the catalogue essays remarks on artists such as the remarkable etcher FL Griggs, and the Neo-Romantics – Sutherland, Piper, Drury, Craxton and Minton – who valued Palmer and showed much of his influence in their work. He was thus kept secure in the affection of later generations.

Oldies on speed!

Single again in her fifties, **MARGARET CRICK** *was persuaded to go Speed Dating – if it was awful, at least it would be over quickly... Illustrations by* **RAY JELLIFFE**

Who would have thought that I'd be going Speed Dating in my fifties? Certainly not me, but then a marriage break-up has changed my life a lot.

'You'll meet somebody else,' said my departing spouse, 'but you'll have to try very hard.'

What an insult! I was sought-after enough before I married, I thought, indignantly. Not a queue of men on bended knee, exactly, but no shortage of admirers. Of course I could still attract men; I just didn't want to have to try hard. But I quickly found out he was right.

During those married years the world has changed. The single men have all but disappeared – they found wives, other men, much younger women, or pubs. Meanwhile, a veritable army of single women has sprung up – resourceful, groomed, available. For those determined to date, the options look extreme: the Internet (scary), lonely-hearts voicemail (expensive), singles clubs (full of single women), matchmaking agencies (ditto), or trusting to fate (hopeless).

'We'll have to go Speed Dating!' says my friend, Monica, who is both blonde and glamorous.

'I've thought of that,' I say, glumly, 'and they don't do it for over-fifties.'

'Yes they do,' she insists. 'I've got a leaflet about it – "Fun event whether you're thirty or sixty." They do it in Bracknell!' Mon is a widow – which gives her status in the cut-throat world of oldie singlehood. Somehow there's still a stigma attached to divorce and separation – though of course only the men can afford to be so choosy. Having said that, Mon is pretty choosy herself – she wants a nice sophisticated man over five-foot eleven so she can wear her gorgeous high-heeled shoes. I'm not so demanding on the height front, but I do insist on OHAT* and GSOH**.

The single men have all but disappeared – they've found wives, other men, much younger women, or pubs

Dressed in our smart casual and not exactly optimistic, we head one evening for Bracknell. It all gets off to a promising start. The Evening (things tend to have Capital Letters in the world of Speed Dating) is held in a private room in a Golf Club and there are quite a few expensive cars in the car park. It costs £12 and no need to book in advance. We are given a number, a pink card with tick-boxes on it, and a handy guide on how to ask questions. Being a journalist, I feel ahead of the game already. We get a drink at the bar and sit at a small table, and other women do the same. After a while a few men self-consciously appear. There are the shy, the nonchalant, the bar hugger, and the prowler – the one who walks round with his coat still on, looking carefully at all the women. 'Definitely NOT!' I mutter to Mon. More men appear, and our spirits lift; this is going to be fun.

To our amazement there are quickly equal numbers of men and women, and the organiser says there would have been even more men but for a football match on telly. That reminds me of another of my requirements: must prefer cricket to football.

The Evening is well-organised and friendly. Jackie is in charge – professional, businesslike, sympathetic (but is she still single?). She explains the system. The men, numbers one to twelve tonight, each sit at a little table and stay put. The female one to twelves move round to each table. We chat, the bell rings, we move on. Three minutes per person. If you like someone, you tick their box on your bit of paper. If they tick yours, it's a Match, but you don't find out till later when you're back home. The suggested questions are for the really cautious: What is your star sign? What is your favourite music? I favour the Tell Me About Yourself approach – guaranteed to fill three minutes with no need to reveal anything much about myself. While I listen, I make little notes: number nine, Paul, smoker; number three, Gareth, ex-wife in Portugal, found time to ask about me; number five, Doug, lives in caravan; number two, Kevin, electronics lecturer, nice-looking. The Prowler turns out to be quite intelligent. At the end of 36 minutes, I'm having great fun. I've ticked three boxes – a gardener, a BT executive, and the electronics lecturer. The range of men, ages and occupations, is large. Most are younger than Mon and me, but we don't feel – or look – out of place, and the atmosphere is jolly.

Our tick-boxes are collected in, and we stand around at the bar chatting. The caravan man has already 'Matched' and is deep in conversation with a woman in a T-shirt. I smile as I pass *en route* to the loo, but she glares back: 'Keep Off!' is the message. You're welcome, is my secret riposte. The Prowler comes to chat to Mon, but is beaten to it by Mr Nice Smile, who has made the mistake of standing up and revealing himself to be a mere five-foot eight.

On the way home, my journalist's notes come in very handy, because by this time we've forgotten who Dave was, what Ian did and whether Chris was too young. We have a giggle remembering our first impressions, but fair's fair, admit there were a few possibles. We now await the Results. In a few days, we should receive a letter telling us which 'gentlemen' we chatted to 'would be delighted' if we made contact with them, together with their contact details. Or maybe we'll get a sad rejection note telling us that, on this occasion, no gentlemen were interested in seeing us again.

Two days later, the organiser's letter duly arrives. I am childishly thrilled to see that five gentlemen (most of them younger than me) have Ticked My Box!

I now have five phone numbers of men who, presumably, fancy me. The momentary euphoria is tempered by seeing that none of them is the gardener, the lecturer or the BT executive. Still, I remember one as being Encouraging and give him a call. Or rather, several calls before I find him in. We arrange to meet for a drink later that week, but a couple of days later he rings to cancel. His mum is having an operation and he must take a few days off to be with her. I half believe it, but that's the last I ever hear from him.

Mon gets five Ticks and a Match. She has ticked Mr Nice Smile and he has ticked her. But the date does not work out. Maybe it's the high-heels problem. Perhaps we are too choosy. But 'He ticks my box' has become our catchphrase. We like a laugh and a night out, so we'll be trying Speed Dating again.

It's fun, it's harmless, and it's a triumph of Hope over Experience – which is what oldie dating is all about!

*Own Hair And Teeth
**Good Sense Of Humour

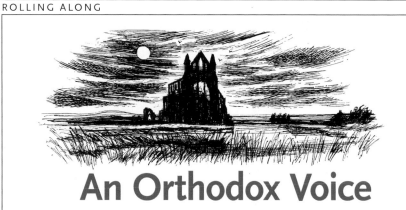

An Orthodox Voice
On The Buses

SOME YEARS ago I gave up owning a car and thereby lost contact with certain classes of people best avoided, *viz.* the police, parking officials, garage workers, insurance men, thieves, vandals, road-ragers and the riff-raff of the highway. The types I now consort with are more congenial – friendly folk who grumble gently at bus stops, kind-hearted bus-drivers and mild-mannered, somewhat enigmatic characters who travel by train. With a free bus pass and senior citizen's rail card I am a man of privilege. And with the money saved I can bridge the gaps in the system, made by Dr Beeching, by recourse to local taxi drivers who are generally thoughtful men with curious or useful information.

Throughout youth and far beyond it I enjoyed a succession of delightful cars, my favourite being a convertible Sunbeam Talbot, a sturdy and sporting roadster. In those days you could park your car anywhere and return weeks later to find it in the same state as when you left it – apart from the flat battery. That was a privilege then, but now everything has been turned round. The days of pleasant motoring are in the past, and you will hardly achieve peace of mind until you are past motoring. Then you can take the bus.

Having lived in the good old days I can affirm that they were no less fearful and painful than the days now present. They were, however, of higher quality. Thinking about the trains and buses of yesteryear, I picture lovingly their lost amenities – the British Rail 4s 6d tea, served by white-gloved stewards in a succession of courses, assorted sandwiches, bread and jam, toasted teacakes, select gateaux – reflecting the common tea-time ritual of those days. And I remember the golden age when buses had roof-racks. On a bicycle journey through ancient Ireland I made much use of local buses. The driver would throw the bike up on the roof, sparing me hours of tedious pedalling.

The big idea of today is that human beings are unreliable and should be replaced by computers. If that were implemented it would entirely destroy the pleasure of travelling. But fortunately it is an impossible fantasy. Buses require drivers, and the best remaining vehicle on which to experience the delights, miseries and adventures of proper, old-fashioned travel is the country bus. It takes ages to get anywhere, of course, and you are liable to be stuck for hours in some unheard-of little town waiting for your connection. Yet those apparent drawbacks are the best part of the system. There are no dull villages in England, nowhere that cannot provide a church, a pub or features of

The big idea of today is that human beings are unreliable and should be replaced by computers

antiquarian or aesthetic interest that you would never have seen were it not for the bus timetable. And when the bus appears, your heart and spirit are uplifted, for you can be sure that something unusual is about to happen. There is no saying what it will be, so the following anecdote is not typical, just a personal memory of a moment of high happiness.

Not so long ago, after smoking had been barred in public transport, I was in Frome, Somerset, travelling west to Shepton Mallet. It was mid-afternoon in summer and I was the only passenger on the Shepton bus. It stopped at several villages but no-one got in, and then the bus became smoky and I saw that the driver had lit up his pipe. That, I assumed, gave me licence to roll up a large cigarette, and we puffed along happily through some of the most beautiful country I have ever seen. I do not remember what happened then, but this incident has reminded me of so many extraordinary bus rides that I am impelled towards an anthology. It would probably be more interesting than, say, *Great Journeys Along The M5*.

JOHN MICHELL

'To be quite honest, I thought drag-hunting meant something else'

Born in the USA

CHARLES GLASS *returned with his daughter to his homeland, but he now views the country like an outsider...*

The Homeland Security officer at Houston airport asked what we were going to do in the United States. I wanted to tell him that it was none of his business. I am a native born citizen. I have studied the Constitution. My family emigrated – or, more likely, were transported – three centuries ago to the North American colonies that are now colonising the world. My daughter, Julia, and I had valid American passports. What the hell was it to him what we did when we came home? However, I did not want to spend the night in an airport slammer, as the son of a friend did recently when a Homeland Security officer took a dislike to him. I gave a coward's reply by telling the truth. We were coming to see my father, her grandfather. He handed back our passports without a word.

'That's nice,' Julia, who is twenty and inherited her American citizenship from me, said. 'You come back to your country, and they treat you like a criminal.'

I wondered whether it really was our country. The Italians used to say that, under Mussolini, the problem was not the big dictator. It was all the little dictators. And, Lord, does America have its share. Men with uniforms

The clothes, the logos, the corporations, the food, the sell, sell, sell... there is no point in leaving America, because America will not leave you

and weapons have, as they say, been empowered. Military hero worship, fuelled by derring-do tales from the badlands of Afghanistan and Iraq, has resurfaced after its premature burial in the killing fields and torture chambers of Vietnam. Citizens are reminded to respect the uniform – of the soldier, the private security guard and the cop. The cop, in the cause of security, can treat the citizen the way soldiers do Muslims in military captivity.

Julia and I flew on to California, where my father has lived all his life apart from five years during and after the war. He votes, as all his forebears since the Civil War have, Republican – although Lincoln might not recognise his party today. A lawyer all his working life, my father still opposes the death penalty. He thinks the country could use some kind of national health service, an un-American beast he and every other American calls, 'socialised medicine'. Despite his opposition to the war in Vietnam, he doesn't mind the war in Iraq. That doesn't bother me as much as seeing him struggle to walk up and down stairs. We stopped arguing politics a long time ago, if only because he grew up in America while I'm growing old in the American empire. Anyway, he's my father, and I understand through him how people at home accept an illegal war, a vicious plutocracy and the shame of being caught red-handed at torture. Life's not bad for them, and they were raised on idealism rather than reality.

The land of the free and home of the brave is swapping freedom for packaged smoke called safety. The state has finally climbed off the backs of honest (that is, rich) businessmen and instead intrudes into our telephone lines, emails and once-privileged relationships between doctors and patients, lawyers and clients, and libraries and their readers. Is this our country? Its owners tell us it's ours, in the way a brothel keeper tells you his house is your home. The deeds to USA, Inc, rest secure in the manicured hands of a few hundred friends and benefactors of George W Bush. The great unwashed are left with television and dreams, perhaps including the elusive American Dream, until they die from the anxiety of meeting their medical bills in old age.

My father told Julia about the war, and his reality was not what Americans learned at school. When the Philippines were liberated from Japan, his ship landed in Manila Bay. He remembered

'Trust me – the old ways are the best'

two things: banners and placards everywhere saying, 'Yankee, go home'; and an American-owned brewery that was the only building in a large area to survive US bombardment. Nothing startling, just not part of the official record. When did you see a Hollywood film whose liberated natives didn't welcome the Americans? (I look forward to *Iraq: The Movie* by DreamWorks, whose wonderfully Freudian name refers to the process of making a terrible dream bearable.) My mother's brother, who died a few years ago, had horror stories about his army unit's treatment of Japanese prisoners of war in Guadalcanal. Julia was too young before he died to hear them, just as most Americans will always be too young to listen to them.

I left America 33 years ago, and it gets harder every year to go back. Julia and the rest of the children were born in London, although they love visiting family in California. Mainly, I go to my father's house and my mother's grave. If they were in Kathmandu, I'd go there. I am American in my bones nonetheless, if only because of my first 21 years of expensive indoctrination. I left in 1972 to see the world for a year or two, but what I came to see was America from afar. I understood at last why Vietnamese peasants put on black pyjamas, lived in underground tunnels and risked their lives to remain Vietnamese rather than let an American impose his idea of freedom on them.

The problem with leaving America is that you can't. It follows you everywhere. If the Marines don't invade your new home, some chain of coffee shops or

Charles Glass (right) with his daughter, Julia and his father

burger bars opens round the corner. The clothes, the canned music, the corporations, the logos, the movies, the food, the cars, the shopping malls, the advertisements, the Weltanschauung – the sell, sell, sell of Babbit-booster culture – find you wherever you hide. There is no point in leaving America, because America will not leave you. Sometimes, you want a rest from everything you grew up with. The salesman's babble – subsidised by the multi-billion dollar bullshit business called Advertising – is relentless.

A few years ago, Norman and Norris Mailer and George Plimpton did a reading of George's play, *Zelda, Scott & Ernest*, at the American Church in Paris. Afterwards, a woman in the audience asked Norman why so many American writers – like Hemingway and Fitzgerald – had moved to Paris. Mailer shrugged and said, 'They probably got tired of being around a lot of stupid people'.

Even other Americans think California is mad, but what happens there travels here. So, get ready for this. We read in the *Los Angeles Times* the story, 'Hoping Canines Will Lap It Up'. A company called K-9 Water of Valencia, California, that sells its product in all fifty states is looking for export markets. As its name hints, it peddles 'flavoured and enriched bottled water for dogs'. The water comes in four flavours: hose water, gutter water, puddle water and toilet water. Susan Goldberg of K-9 Water says, 'The doggie business is just exploding with dog resorts and dog spas'. She said a friend of hers was opening a chain of 'dog-friendly coffee shops' to be called Pawbucks (I am not making this up). The paper added that 43 per cent of America's dog owners celebrate Fido's birthday. Perhaps the other 57 per cent make do with Christmas presents from a doggy toy manufacturer called Paws 'n More.

My brother-in-law, at whose house we were staying, told me that dog food has overtaken the sales of baby food. An old English professor of mine predicted back in 1968 that human beings would die out and only dogs would be left. It seems to be going that way. K-9 Water comes from the people who are exporting democracy to an Arab world that regards dogs as 'unclean' and won't allow them indoors. Those American dogs may have to blast their way in.

Being single is great...

you can head for the seaside

then change your mind... and go back home

GED

Crewe Station, Cheshire

Left: 'Blues at Crewe' circa 1959. Painting by Mike Turner G R A

O h Mr Porter what shall I do? I wanted to go to Birmingham But they sent me on to Crewe. Despite the jokes about delays at Crewe, despite working out anagrams of Crewe Station and coming up with 'Train woes, etc.', for me it is still a thrilling station to visit. It is a trainspotter's paradise, it is what Dungeness is to twitchers.

Set amidst lush Cheshire dairy country, Crewe remains the most romantic and practical railway town in the world. Look at it on a map and you will see the railway lines striking across Middle England towards it from six different directions. It looks like the middle of a snowflake under a magnifying glass.

In 1837, it was merely a small stop between Warrington and Birmingham. At the point where the line crossed the turnpike road linking the Trent and Mersey and the Shropshire Union Canals, the railway developers bought land from the Earl of Crewe, and called the junction 'Crewe'. With the opening of the Grand Junction Railway on 4th July 1837, Crewe began to make world history: it was the first place to have its own railway hotel; the first place to form a junction between more than two companies; and the first place to have a completely independent railway system

> **For me, it is still a thrilling station to visit. It is a trainspotter's paradise, it is what Dungeness is to twitchers**

built around it to ease traffic congestion.

The Grand Junction Railway's purpose was to link the four largest cities in England by joining the existing Liverpool and Manchester Railway with the projected London and Birmingham railway. The line, the first long-distance railway in the world, ran from Curzon Street station in Birmingham to Dallam in Warrington.

When the station opened, it was seen as a useful point to begin a branch line to the county town of Chester. A locomotive depot was built to provide banking engines to assist trains southwards from Crewe up the Madeley Incline.

In 1842, the Grand Junction Railway moved its locomotive works to Crewe and more houses were built for the workforce. By 1861, the station had to be re-built to cope with the increased traffic. The town further expanded under the leadership of John Ramsbottom, the locomotive superintendent for what had now become the North Western Railway Company – the largest railway

company in the world. In 1871, he was succeeded by Frank Webb, a vicar's son, who became known as 'the uncrowned King of Crewe'. By the 1890s, Crewe had 1,000 trains passing through it a day, and the town's population was nearing 50,000. In 1903, another legendary railway man, George Whale, took over from Webb, but Crewe's power and glory could not last forever. With the passing of steam, trains did not need to stop at Crewe to change locomotives. Myriad branch railways were axed and fewer trains terminated at Crewe. In 1985 the entire track layout was modernised, simplified and reduced.

'Hi Derek. I'm on the seat behind you'

Beauty and the freak show

JOAN RHODES *used to perform as a strong woman. She tore a telephone book in half and bent iron bars with her teeth, and once dropped Bob Hope on his head...*

The Hackney Empire was slowly dying by the time I got there for the first time in 1949. I had been very strong as a child, and after I'd left home at the age of 14 I saw a strong man performing outside the National Portrait Gallery, offered to take the hat round, and – to his and my surprise – bent one of his six-inch nails in half. After working as a dancer in Spain, I answered an ad for 'Freaks Wanted'. 'You don't look like a freak,' I was told when I went for an interview, so I tore up the interviewer's phone book and carried him round the office – and got the job.

At the Empire I was in a show called *Would You Believe It?* in which the 'Wonders of the World' could be seen – among them two giants, one seven feet three inches and the other over nine feet tall, having a mock boxing match with a dwarf as the referee. Then there was Elroy, the 'Armless Wonder' – he really didn't have any arms, yet there on stage, before your very eyes, he painted Rolf Harris-style pictures. He shot at a target, threaded needles, and had the best foot-writing I ever saw. He was a lovely man. Once he caught me coming downstairs, put his leg round my waist and said, 'You're a pretty thing.' He liked to sit on a stool in the pub, order a pint, take out his purse and pick up his pint with his mittened foot, which had been beautifully manicured by his faithful help, George, a tiny, busy man who arranged everything for him and hardly ever spoke – at least within my hearing.

Mushie the 'Forest-Bred Lion', who ate steaks off a lady's forehead, was also on the bill. Every night, when his cage was drawn away, poor old Mushie was left standing, chained and centre-stage. He used to face the auditorium and pee against the backcloth. He was

I tore up the 'Freak Show' interviewer's phone book and carried him around the office – and got the job

presented to audiences by Captain Jack Harvey, dressed like a great white hunter, who had been in the jungle since the days before Mushie was born. I remember the Captain wore the most amazing red ochre make-up.

Then there was Pelletier and Partner, the 'World's Only Dog's Dancing Partner', and Johnny Vree, billed as a 'Dutch Porter', who threw what appeared to be a large golliwog around the stage and then tried to get it back in its box. At the end of the act, the golliwog would remove its mask, revealing a beautiful girl, six feet tall and very slender. Reco and May were a comedy wire act: he did amazing things on a slack wire, dressed as a clown, while she shouted encouragement and caught him when he fell off (all beautifully rehearsed). Bob Andrews, billed as 'Genial Generalities', was the compère. He had a beautiful singing voice, and knew every gag in the business: they hadn't been spoiled by repetition on TV, so every one seemed new.

Whoever arrived first at the theatre would run through the music. We used to perform twice nightly, at 6.30pm and again at 8.40pm. By six, most artists were arranging the props for their own acts – your lighting plot had been given out, and the stage manager informed of your needs while the band tuned up and the artists warmed up. I liked a dark backcloth, with maybe a lilac or a rose pink swag, a small table, and four chairs. I would invite the four strongest men to come on stage. For a moment I wondered whether anyone would take up my offer, but then they rushed up to help. I must have had good legs in those days! Known as the 'Mighty Mannequin', I used to tear telephone directories in half and bend iron bars with my teeth. King Farouk used to send me tiger lilies, and once asked me if I would break his bed in two. I replied 'Not tonight, Josephine!'

I was usually in the second half of the show, so I had time to peak through a crack in the curtains and watch the people come in and the theatre coming alive, all bright with coloured lights,

Joan has always thought herself lucky

plenty of gold leaf and lots of red velvet. Having paid their half-crowns, the public were ready to enjoy themselves. Smart usherettes sold two-penny programmes, there was the rustle of chocolate boxes being opened, a tap of the baton, and the show was on.

The public were very loyal, and if they liked you, they let you know. but if they didn't, they would sit on their hands. A whole family would see a two-hour show for a pound, wandering off afterwards to eat fish and chips from yesterday's newspaper.

Then came the big names from America: Johnny Ray, Bob Hope, the Deep River Boys and countless others whose names I can't recall – though I do remember dropping Bob Hope on his head. They demanded so much money that only half the bill was 'variety', and the 'star' would stay on stage for a whole hour. Prices went up to pay the stars, and TV was on its way. Variety acts only lasted between 12 and 15 minutes, and if the old man didn't care for an act he could pop out to the bar for a pint – but acts that lasted a whole hour were a very different matter. So let's have some good variety back again – though it will be difficult to find good acts at first, because the best are now Continental.

I once met...
Lord Boothby

Photograph courtesy of Getty Images

For many years, my principle claim to fame was that I had been farted at by Lord Boothby. The events leading up to this are as follows.

In 1967 I had a summer job as night porter at the four-star Newton Hotel in Nairn. There was great excitement among the staff as rumours spread that Lord Boothby and his new bride were to spend their honeymoon at the hotel.

Although known to the world then as Baron Boothby of Buchan and Rattray Head, I had been aware of him many years before as Bob Boothby, MP, a doughty fighter for all things pertaining to his constituency in North East Scotland. The only clue was an entry in the hotel diary concerning the arrival on a certain date of 'Mr and Mrs Honeyman'.

The date arrived and so did the Boothbys – Lord Boothby, the charming new Lady Boothby, a native of Sardinia, and the chauffeur of their far from new Renault car, who seemed to do everything with them.

On the night in question, dinner had been taken, as had a considerable amount of Lord Boothby's tipple, a liqueur called Kummel. I was behind the night porter's desk as the party came into view to retrieve their keys. I realised that his lordship was looking straight at me as he neared, with his characteristic expression of a pugilist whose cauliflower ear had extended to take in most of his face.

He stopped and, still looking straight at me, emitted the blast as described in the opening sentence.

Had I been asked in advance, I would have expected a thing from such a man to be majestic, in the nature of a MacBrayne's ferry half-way up the Sound of Mull announcing its arrival to the population of Tobermory: but no, it was high-pitched and variable in note. In the context of Victor Borge's phonetic punctuation, it was a question mark with a hint of gothic in the architecture.

...with his characteristic expression of a pugilist whose cauliflower ear had extended over most of his face

His lordship continued to look straight at me, and growled one word: 'Owzat?' With hindsight I should have adopted the cricket umpire's role, raised a finger and said, in a grand manner, 'Out'.

Alas, all I could do, quivering menial that I was, was to compliment him on his effort and hand over the keys.

GORDON COOK

The New Secretary

An unsettling idyll

PENELOPE BENNETT *wonders what it is about Simon Palmer's paintings*
that makes them so beautiful, yet so disconcerting...

Who is the painter of this intriguing, almost hypnotic painting? He is Simon Palmer, born in Doncaster in 1956, educated at Reigate School of Art, where he intended specialising in illustration until his tutors advised him to concentrate on drawing and painting the Kentish countryside instead.

'Had I,' he says, 'studied fine art, I would probably not be painting now.'

He paints mainly in watercolour, gouache and ink, describing his style as both narrative and allegorical. Since 1986 he has lived in Ellingstring, North Yorkshire.

Something less easy to define, something eerie makes me want to step back to the other side of Palmer's picture frame

As with other Palmer paintings, *The New Secretary* immediately makes me want to step into its idyllic bosky landscape, with its fields knee-deep in sunshine, its velvety shadows thick enough to hold in the hands... But then something less easy to define, something eerie, makes me want to step back to the other side of the picture frame.

Why has the new secretary come to a standstill in the middle of the road? There's a touching vulnerability about her stillness and thinness, as there is about many of Palmer's figures. Is she anxious about her new job, the cows-crossing road sign, or the intimidating black shadows she will have to wade through? Simon Palmer's pictures make one ask many questions to which, perhaps fortunately, there are few answers.

His woolly-foliaged trees, present in most of his work, could be embroidered or woven. 'Trees,' he says, 'are wonderful. Our tallest natural plants, they outlive us by generations. Their roots plunge deep into the earth. It's what lies beneath the thin crust we call landscape that holds the clues to our surroundings. Trees seem to tap into this and link the two together.'

Palmer's work is held in numerous collections in Europe, America and Japan. He has undertaken commissions for the National Trust at Sissinghurst and at Salt's Mill, Saltaire. In May 1995 he was voted 'Most Creative Artist' by the *Independent*.

The case of the 34 dead fish

I've had it with fish. No sooner are they brought back from Squires and deposited in our fish tank, than they lose the will to live. The death toll so far is 34. And it is not my fault. I'm just unlucky with fish. My tank is cleaned regularly, treated with a special solution to stop the fish from being stressed (I ask you), and thoughtfully furnished with a model ancient ruin, a floor of the finest gravel, a filter, and water plant to nibble on. Frankly, there's no excuse for not living.

The other day I went with my eight-year-old daughter Betty to buy two new fish. Betty pointed to the ones she quite liked the look of, and as Gary from Squires inserted the net to scoop them out, I let it slip about the death toll. I even made a little joke about me being an aquatic version of Dr Shipman, but Gary did not think this was funny. He took the news very badly indeed. He immediately whisked the empty net out of the water and stared at me. 'What's wrong?' I asked nervously.

'I'm sorry madam,' said Gary, 'but I can't sell you any fish until you find out why the others died.' I was taken aback. 'But we've come all this way,' I protested.

'I'm sorry,' said Gary, 'but it would be irresponsible to sell you more fish until you've identified the problem. I must consider the welfare of the fish.'

He asked me if there might be something wrong with the water. Affronted, I told him it was as clean as Evian. 'How do you know?'

he asked. 'Because I always put that anti-stress stuff in which also kills the chlorine.' 'That's not enough,' said Gary. 'You've got to test it regularly for levels of ammonia and nitrate.' He paused. 'Have you tested it, madam?' It was then I told a lie. 'Yes,' I said, flushing. Gary asked how. My eyes darted around the shelves, desperately searching for water-testing kits I could name, but all I could see were nautical ornaments. 'With a stick thing,' I blurted. 'A stick thing?' 'Yes, you put it in the water and it beeps if it's not right. I bought it in Calais...' I added, bizarrely. Gary said he hadn't heard of such a kit, and advised me to bring in a water sample for testing. I reluctantly agreed, and left fish-less, and humiliated.

On the way home I remembered the lady in Squires' pet department who once gaily told me about the customer who buys baby rabbits to feed to his pet python. Why, I asked Betty, was it okay for Python Man to feed live rabbits to his snake, and not all right for me to take pot luck with a couple of £2.50 goldfish? Betty said she didn't know, and to stop talking about fish.

I can't bring myself to buy a water-testing kit, and I don't want Gary have the satisfaction of finding the water in my tank contains a dangerously high level of nitrate or, worse, alcohol from the time when Mr Shopping tripped over the dog and his Stella Artois went everywhere.

ALICE PITMAN

'I'm leaving you, Brian, this addiction to selling things on eBay has gone too far!'

THE OFFICERS' ASSOCIATION RESIDENTIAL HOME
'Huntly'

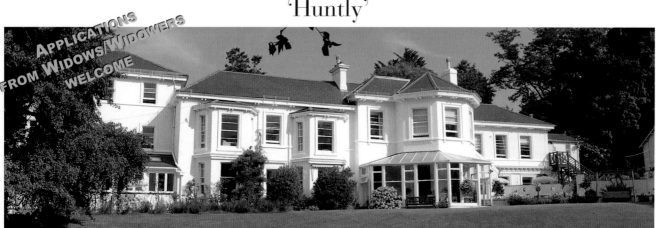

APPLICATIONS FROM WIDOWS/WIDOWERS WELCOME

LOCATED ON THE OUTSKIRTS OF NEWTON ABBOT IN SOUTH DEVON

"HUNTLY" IS THE OFFICERS' ASSOCIATION'S RESIDENTIAL RETIREMENT HOME FOR ELDERLY SINGLE EX-OFFICERS, MALE OR FEMALE, OF ALL THREE SERVICES, AND WIDOWS AND WIDOWERS OF EX-OFFICERS WHO WISH TO ENJOY AN ACTIVE RETIREMENT IN A PEACEFUL AND TRANQUIL ENVIRONMENT. LOCATED IN THE VILLAGE OF BISHOPSTEIGNTON AND SITUATED IN ITS OWN EXTENSIVE LANDSCAPED GROUNDS, SOUTH FACING OVER THE TEIGN ESTUARY, HUNTLY OFFERS THE COMFORT, SECURITY AND PEACE OF MIND OF A COMMUNITY WHILE PRESERVING THE INDEPENDENCE AND PRIVACY OF ITS INDIVIDUAL RESIDENTS. ALL RESIDENTS HAVE A SINGLE ROOM, MOST WITH EN-SUITE FACILITIES AND THE SPACIOUS PUBLIC ROOMS INCLUDE A DINING ROOM, DRAWING ROOM, LIBRARY, SNOOKER ROOM, ANTEROOM AND TWO TV ROOMS. THE CLIMATE IS NOTABLY MILD AND DRY, BEING ON THE ENGLISH RIVIERA. FAST COMMUNICATIONS BY BOTH ROAD AND RAIL ARE CONVENIENTLY CLOSE.

APPLICANTS MUST BE MOBILE, ABLE TO LOOK AFTER THEMSELVES AND ATTEND MEALS. THERE ARE NO MEDICAL FACILITIES AT HUNTLY, ALTHOUGH THE LOCAL DOCTOR VISITS EACH WEEK AND WELFARE OFFICERS ARE EMPLOYED TO PROVIDE SUPPORT FOR THE RESIDENTS. ALL RESIDENTS PAY A STANDARD FEE THAT COVERS THEIR ACCOMMODATION, MEALS AND WELFARE SUPPORT.

CONTACT THE ASSISTANT GENERAL SECRETARY ON
Tel: 0845 873 7142 Email: AGSPA@OAED.ORG.UK
The Officers Association, 1st Floor Mountbarrow House, 6-20 Elizabeth Street, London, SW1W 9RB
OR VISIT OUR WEBSITE: WWW.OFFICERSASSOCIATION.ORG.UK FOR FURTHER DETAILS AND A COLOUR BROCHURE AND APPLICATION FORM.

Just fancy that!

The vile **WILFRED DE'ATH** *was asked to join his housing association committee and organise a fancy-dress party. How did they cope with his lurid costume suggestions?*

It's the fiftieth anniversary of the founding of the St Pancras and Humanist Housing Association which owns and runs the old-people sheltered retirement block in Cambridge, where I live. In honour of the occasion, they decided to give a fancy-dress party – the 1950s – and just guess who was invited to organise the costumes? Yours truly!

My life to date has been filled with fantastic and, if I'm honest, somewhat unrealistic ambitions. I once thought of getting ordained into the Church of England and, had I done so, I don't doubt that I would have made Archbishop of Canterbury. Then I thought of becoming a theatre director and am convinced that I would have ended up running the National. I eventually became a BBC radio producer at the age of 23, and I'm equally sure I would have controlled Radio 4, had I stayed around. At present, I'm working at winning the Nobel Prize for Literature.

However, of all these failed honours, nothing compares with the excitement of being co-opted on to the Entertainment Committee of the St Pancras and Humanist Housing Association. Would this prove to be my finest hour?

My first committees were not terribly encouraging. An ancient crone (87) wasted the first twenty minutes with her irrelevant reminiscences of the 1950s. Toni, our gorgeous manageress, took offence when I suggested she should come to the party as Sandy, the 'leather-clad tart' from *Grease* (I was obliged to offer flowers and apologies at the next meeting).

You'd think we were renegotiating Britain's entry into the European Union, not trying to provide a pleasant afternoon for oldies

A cadaverous oldie known only as 'Long John' similarly resented being cast as Danny, the John Travolta role from the same film (since he usually spends most of his life, dressed as a woman, I thought it would make a nice change for him). Our statuesque deputy warden, Jill, didn't like being told (by yours truly, again) that she ought to come as a Hattie Jacques 1950s-type hospital matron (more flowers, more apologies).

Committee followed committee at regular intervals over what seemed like months. You'd think we were renegotiating Britain's entry into the European Union, not trying to provide a pleasant afternoon for a houseful of OAPs.

The party, when the great day finally arrived, was a bit of an anticlimax. Taking pleasure in dressing up as somebody else has always struck me as being a sign of immaturity (you're only young once, but you can be immature at any age). I found it interesting to see that the more eccentric the pensioner, the better and more exotic his/her costume turned out to be.

Alf, a hopeless, broken-down case, made a fabulous 1950s' 'spiv' – the kind of man who used to sell stolen horses at country fairs. He got my first prize. Then Henry, another boozer, with a university degree, came as a 1950s' schoolmaster complete with gown and frayed Harris Tweed jacket. He came second. Toni, in the end, didn't disappoint, and came as Sandy. And yours truly? Well, as all the world knows, I am a juvenile delinquent trapped in the body of a 68-year-old career criminal. So I came as myself.

I once met...
Enoch Powell

Enoch Powell wasn't much of a customer. His wife was the one who spent the money, regularly buying kitchen utensils and garden tools from my father's ironmongers shop in Wolverhampton's Chapel Ash.

During its final years the shop's trade had declined and my father ran the place alone. From time to time he'd ask me to take over so that he could enjoy a much needed weekend break. It was towards the end of a dismal November day and I was looking forward to closing up and heading homewards. There had been no customers since half past five and, as I began to cash up at ten to six, rain fell steadily in the darkness outside. There were rarely any customers during the last half-hour of the day and I often wondered why my father never closed the shop earlier. It was years after that I realised the shop's closing time coincided with the opening of The Clarendon, only a step away, where Dad invariably put a full stop to the day's business.

I was locking the back door when the phone rang. I answered to hear the unmistakable tones of Enoch Powell. He had a curious accent – what I can only describe as 'posh Wolverhampton'.

'Don't close yet,' he ordered me. 'I'll be there in five minutes.'

I was very young and he was a distinguished statesman, so I did as I was told. By five past six I decided he wasn't coming, so I switched off the lights and made for the front door, which I'd locked while counting the day's takings. As I reached it there was a loud tapping on the glass. The prominent eyes of Enoch Powell peered from his pale face into the gloom within. His moustache quivered with urgency and water streamed from the broad rim of his black Homburg hat. Reluctantly I let him in and locked the door behind him, wondering what was so urgent it was worth braving such foul weather. He marched up to the counter, pulled a green-stained brass garden tap from the pocket of his heavy overcoat and placed it in front of me. 'It needs a new washer,' he said, flatly.

'We need a vice,' he said. 'You must have one in here somewhere.'

I turned on the lights again and asked him what sort of washer it needed. He didn't know; he couldn't get the thing apart. Great, I thought. After several minutes of futile struggle – a sort of arm-wrestling match with Mr Powell holding the tap in a large wrench while I heaved on an equally large spanner, I gave up. 'It's not going to shift,' I said. 'You'd be better off with a new tap.' Enoch Powell, however, gave up less easily.

'We need a vice,' he said. 'You must have one in here somewhere.'

I should have replied with a categorical 'No'. Instead, I hesitated. 'Not really... There's a very old thing upstairs, but...'

He jumped on this eagerly. I explained that there was no light on the top floor; electricity had never been installed beyond the first flight of stairs. In fact, the upper storey was now used for the storage of unwanted clutter; piles of dusty hessian sacks, broken and unrepaired tools, and several life-sized cardboard figures bearing cheerful smiles as they demonstrated some new product or other. Many years ago, the front room of the top floor had been a workshop. The bench my grandfather once used was still there but it now leaned awkwardly at a sharp angle since one of its legs had become detached. The vice was completely rusted over but eventually I managed to open its jaws and, while Enoch held the torch, I tightened them on the resisting tap. Slowly I prised it apart. I picked up the pieces and, taking the torch from Enoch's hand, led the return to the ground floor, periodically shedding the light behind me. It wasn't so much courtesy as a desire not to be crushed to death by a falling Enoch Powell.

Behind the counter, on a high shelf reached only by the small wooden ladder kept for the purpose, was a box of leather washers. I climbed up and brought it down. Inside, the box was partitioned by interlocking cardboard dividers into 24 small compartments, each containing a different size or shape of washer. On the underside of the lid was a diagram replicating its contents with a brief description of each item – three-quarter-inch cup, half-inch heavy duty, etc. Unfortunately, the compartment that should have contained washers of the sort needed was empty. Somehow, I wasn't surprised.

Mr Powell reached into the box and picked out one of the three-quarter-inch cup washers. 'This should do it,' he said. 'It just needs trimming to shape.'

So, naturally, that's what I did. I took up a Stanley knife and trimmed the cup-shaped flange until I'd achieved a three-quarter-inch flat washer – more or less.

I squeezed it into the tap, reassembled the various bits and handed the product of half an hour's labour to what I assumed to be a highly satisfied customer.

'How much do I owe you?' he asked.

I peered at the lid of the box where prices had been written, probably by my grandfather 25 years earlier.

It read '6d' – six pence in old money.

I should have said six shillings but I was anticipating a handsome tip.

'Sixpence,' I replied.

And that's what he gave me – sixpence – not a penny more.

DAVID THOMAS

DOES SITTING MAKE YOUR BACK ACHE?

The MEDesign Backfriend relieves back pain

- More than 600,000 used in 35 countries
- Light and portable, for use in any seat
- Height adjustable back
- Available in 7 colours
- 12 month guarantee
- Made in UK by MEDesign® Ltd

at Home

Driving

Relaxing

Working

Backfriend

Anywhere

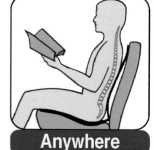
Praying

Leaf blowers on the line

CHARLES ELLIOTT *loves his leaf blower, but he's in a minority. Why are they so hated?*

Does anybody enjoy raking leaves? Very few gardening activities can be quite so boring, exhausting, and pointless. But it must be done.

We have an exceptional number of trees, all of which – even the larches – insist on shedding their leaves as winter approaches. So I have become the owner of a leaf blower.

It wasn't the first piece of garden machinery I've bought. I have quite a collection – a string trimmer, a chainsaw, a hedge clipper, a rototiller, and several mowers. I frankly delight in them. They save a vast amount of time and labour. Purists might argue that I'm missing some of the perks concomitant to hand work – that sense of ecstatic close-to-the-earth weariness granted to those who have put in a solid day's toil with a hoe. But if weariness is the issue, I don't have any problem getting weary lifting a twenty-pound hedge clipper over sixty yards of hedge.

I got my leaf blower towards the end of last autumn, having already collected most of the year's leaves with a rake. I used it only a few times, to corral some late-descending leaves and see if it might clear the grass cuttings inadvertently sprayed on the gravel drive by the lawnmower. It worked all too well on the drive – it blew both grass cuttings and a substantial proportion of the gravel straight back onto the lawn. As for the leaves, the main problem was getting them into a pile, since the blower functioned rather like a stiff northeast wind, with the same degree of discrimination. Before long it went into winter storage.

Leaf blowers are a fairly recent invention. The first time I saw one I couldn't figure out what it was. That was in about 1990 in a large hardware store in Troy, New York. I've seldom seen them in Britain; Monnow Mowers and Machinery in Monmouth, where I got mine, has been carrying them for only a few years. So I decided to do some leaf blower research. What I discovered makes me wonder whether I'll ever have the nerve to use it again. This is a machine in very deep controversy, if not worse.

According to most sources, leaf blowers were invented by Japanese engineers in the 1970s, and originally used to blow fertilizers and pesticides over fruit trees and grain fields. A container of chemicals sat atop a powerful fan, to be blasted in the general direction of a needy crop through a nozzle. One day somebody discovered that even without the chemicals, the blast of air alone could be of use, and the leaf blower was born. Imaginative

Leaf blowers are not much loved. In fact, in many places in the USA, they are not even tolerated

manufacturers have since come up with more uses for the machine, such as blowing snow, clearing rain gutters, cleaning parking lots and sports arenas, 'dislodging matted grass' (whatever that is), 'drying lawns', and, of course, gathering leaves. Some leaf blowers, I learn, can be made to run backwards, thus creating a kind of outdoor Hoover.

Now, while this range of practical applications doesn't make the machines a benefit to humanity on the level of, say, penicillin or mains electricity, it does suggest that most people would regard them as admirable. Thus I was surprised to find that leaf blowers are not much loved. In fact, in many places in the United States they are not even tolerated. Today, six out of the ten largest California cities either ban leaf blowers outright or place severe restrictions on their use. This in spite of the fact that, according

to the latest figures I can find (1999), something like one million petrol and electric leaf blowers have been sold in California alone. Nor can leaf-blower rage be written off as a peculiarly Californian phenomenon. New Jersey and Arizona have both considered state-level laws against the machines, while prosperous Montgomery County in Maryland has had a restrictive law on the books for 15 years. Five other states have at least one city with a leaf blower ordinance.

What's the fuss? One objection is the amount of dust – laden with everything from pollen to pesticides – that leaf blowers create. Then there are the engine emissions; a two-stroke engine spews nearly a third of its fuel unburned into the air. But the heart of the problem is noise.

It is difficult to describe the sound of a leaf blower at full throttle. It is a sort of deep, hollow roar that wraps itself around your spine and causes the synapses to misfire. Wearing ear protectors is not only a good idea, it's imperative.

Most of the ordinances controlling leaf blowers (as opposed to banning them) specify that the noise they make should be limited to 65 decibels at fifty feet, variously described as 'the sound of an alarm clock' or 'freeway traffic.' The average leaf blower emits roughly 110 decibels, a great deal more than twice as loud; a car horn, a pneumatic drill, or somebody shouting in your ear registers about 110 decibels. Experts claim that extended exposure (more than eight hours) to as little as 85 decibels is likely to cause damage to one's hearing.

At the moment, my leaf blower is hanging in the barn, gleaming quietly, its red plastic nozzle ready to roar at the pull of a starter cord. Autumn is approaching, and my enthusiasm for raking is at a serious ebb. The temptation to get out there and blow will, I know, be extremely powerful. Monmouthshire has made no move towards banning the machine, so I won't be breaking any laws. The question is: should I? I suggest you listen carefully come October. You'll probably be able to hear the answer.

Going over the top

Like many a good read, Robert Graves's classic First World War memoir, Goodbye to All That, *turns out to have been economical with the truth, says* **A D HARVEY**

Robert Graves is one of those poets whom everyone knows by reputation but whose poetry few people have read. His critical writings, wespecially *The White Goddess*, seem now to have little more than curiosity value. His novels *I Claudius* and *Wife to Mr Milton* helped establish the intimately debunking what-silly-underwear-the-field-marshal-is-wearing school of historical fiction, though Gore Vidal subsequently produced better work of this type.

The one book by Robert Graves that is likely to be much read 100 years from now is his memoir of youth and war service, *Goodbye to All That*, published 75 years ago this month.

Graves later admitted, 'I have more or less deliberately mixed in all the ingredients that I know are mixed into other popular books, specifically food and drink, murders, ghosts, kings, one's mother, T E Lawrence and the Prince of Wales.' He was fortunate enough to have had a one-to-one encounter with the future Duke of Windsor in a public bath at Bethune – His Royal Highness 'graciously remarked how bloody cold the water was' – and he knew T E Lawrence well enough to ask him for a reference when applying for a professorship in Cairo, but it was his four years as a subaltern on the Western Front which provided him with his best material.

Goodbye to All That is one of those books which is impossible to put down. It provides a far more vivid sense of the British Army as an organism, or organisation, with its own distinctive internal economy, than any other of the literary classics of the First World War. Whether the picture it gives is an accurate one is another matter.

The Berg Collection in the New York Public Library has a copy in which Siegfried Sassoon and Edmund Blunden marked various factual errors; a couple of others are indicated in the copy formerly owned by Captain J C Dunn, the Medical Officer of Graves's battalion, and now in possession of the Royal Welch Fusiliers,

though Dunn usually confined himself to scribbling in the margins remarks like 'rot', 'fiction', 'bunkum' or, in one instance, 'a good deal of this para is astray'. Since then, the release of wartime records at the National Archives has enabled me to check some of Graves's most striking statements.

He claimed, for example, that officers who stayed too long in the trenches often became dipsomaniacs. 'I knew three or

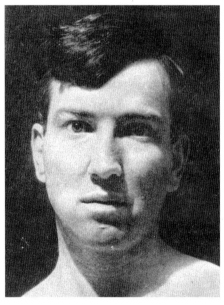

Graves had reputedly the largest feet in the Army, and a genius for putting both of them in everything

four who had worked up to the point of two bottles [of whisky] a day before being lucky enough to get wounded or sent home in some other way. A two-bottle company commander of one of our line battalions is still alive who, in three shows running, got his company needlessly destroyed because he was no longer capable of taking clear decisions.'

It is somewhat suspicious, to say the least, that Graves wrote this at the height of the controversy over R C Sherriff's play *Journey's End*, which had an alcoholic company commander as one of its protagonists, and though

the 'two-bottle company commander' whom Graves referred to was identified in Captain Dunn's marginal notes as Captain R C J Greaves, when the latter applied for transfer to the Royal Flying Corps the only thing mentioned against him in his personal file was that he needed glasses.

Graves was scathing, too, about the reluctance of the Church of England chaplains to risk their lives in the forward trenches, and the superior reputation enjoyed by Roman Catholic chaplains, and told the story of Father Gleeson of the Munsters who 'when all the officers were killed or wounded at the first battle of Ypres, had stripped off his black badges and, taking command of the survivors, held the line'. For some unaccountable reason there is no allusion to this incident in Captain McCance's two-volume history of the Royal Munster Fusiliers, though Father Gleeson is mentioned six times in his ecclesiastical capacity, and the unit war diary in the National Archives indicates that at the First Battle of Ypres the Munsters suffered relatively fewer losses among the officers than among the other ranks.

It also turns out that all three of the army chaplains who won the VC in the First World War for tending men under fire were in Church of England orders: one of them, the Rev T B Hardy, VC, DSO, MC, who died of wounds complicated by pneumonia in October 1918 at the age of 52, was described by his battalion adjutant as 'the most wonderful man I have ever met'. Graves, on the other hand, was described by Captain Dunn, the medical officer of his battalion, as having 'reputedly the largest feet in the Army, and a genius for putting both of them in everything'.

But then, young men with a genius for ingratiating themselves with the older officers in their regiment seldom write the sort of biography one would want to read at a sitting.

Photograph of the young Robert Graves from the original edition of *Goodbye to All That*

'Frankly, your bum looks big in anything'